The Radical Gospel of
Bishop Thomas Gumbleton

Credit: *National Catholic Reporter*/Arthur Jones

The Radical Gospel of Bishop Thomas Gumbleton

Peter Feuerherd

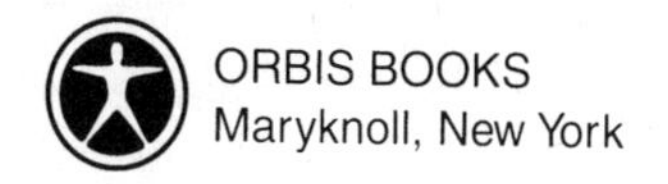

Founded in 1970, Orbis Books endeavors to publish works that enlighten the mind, nourish the spirit, and challenge the conscience. The publishing arm of the Maryknoll Fathers and Brothers, Orbis seeks to explore the global dimensions of the Christian faith and mission, to invite dialogue with diverse cultures and religious traditions, and to serve the cause of reconciliation and peace. The books published reflect the views of their authors and do not represent the official position of the Maryknoll Society. To learn more about Maryknoll and Orbis Books, please visit our website at www.maryknollsociety.org.

Published by Orbis Books, Box 302, Maryknoll, NY 10545-0302.

Manufactured in the United States of America

Library of Congress Cataloging-in-Publication Data

Names: Feuerherd, Peter, author.
Title: The radical gospel of Bishop Thomas Gumbleton / Peter Feuerherd.
Description: Maryknoll, NY : Orbis Books, [2019]
Identifiers: LCCN 2019015266 (print) | LCCN 2019018899 (ebook) | ISBN 9781608337613 (ebook) | ISBN 9781626983403 (pbk.)
Subjects: LCSH: Gumbleton, Thomas J. | Catholic Church—United States—Bishops—Biography. | Catholic Church—United States—History—20th century.
Classification: LCC BX4705.G8433 (ebook) | LCC BX4705.G8433 F48 2019 (print) | DDC 282.092—dc23
LC record available at https://lccn.loc.gov/2019015266

To Mercedes, who every day offers me a look at the radical gospel.

Contents

Credit: Rick Reinhard

Chapter 1

A Different Kind of Bishop

> *"Leaders are not people who simply conform to what somebody else tells them."*

Why a biography of an American Catholic bishop? At this time? Those are natural questions to ask, as these words are written, following what has been a horrific year for many Catholics, and for others who wish to view the church as a moral guidepost.

As far as the reputation of bishops went, 2018 seemed to be a nadir. Over the summer, a nearly one-thousand-page report detailing sex abuse crimes and cover-ups in virtually all the dioceses of Pennsylvania was released by a grand jury. The details were sickening. One priest was said to have had sexual relations with five sisters in a family he befriended; another group of priests was said to have passed around boys who were routinely marked with identifiers, including crucifixes. In the pages of this report Catholics heard about bishops who tried to push these events away from the glare of public scrutiny and law enforcement. Some described the events as satanic, a word rarely invoked but perhaps the only adequate description.

There was nothing unique about Pennsylvania. It seemed likely that other places, if examined thoroughly, would surely reveal the same patterns of wrongdoing and cover-up. Attorneys general in New York, New Jersey, and Missouri, among other states, threatened to conduct similar investigations into both contemporary cases and others from decades ago.

The Pennsylvania revelations were coupled with the case of eighty-eight-year-old Cardinal Theodore McCarrick, former archbishop of Washington, DC, now retired, who was accused of molesting an altar boy while serving in the Archdiocese of New York back in the early 1970s. Other revelations followed. The *New York Times* uncovered agreements signed with two New Jersey dioceses where McCarrick had served as bishop, Metuchen and Newark, involving payments to former seminarians who had accused him of sexual harassment. Meanwhile, old rumors about McCarrick's behavior toward seminarians in New Jersey surfaced. As archbishop of Newark, McCarrick was said to have brought seminarians to a beach house on the Jersey shore. The scheme was a regular pattern: He would invite more seminarians than there were beds in the house. He would then "have to" share a bed with one of the seminarians.

And then there was the onslaught from Archbishop Carlo Maria Viganò, former nuncio, or ambassador, for the Vatican to the United States. He attacked the widely beloved Pope Francis, saying that the pope himself had known of McCarrick's reputation, and that Pope Benedict had suspended McCarrick from acting as a clergyman. (This despite the fact that McCarrick never seemed to honor any suspension, traveling the world on various fund-raising and diplomatic causes, even being greeted with honor by Pope Benedict and Viganò himself at public functions.)

This was a complicated, disheartening mess. And throughout that summer, via phone linkups to the staffers at the *National Catholic Reporter* (*NCR*) in Kansas City, Missouri, and around the world, I participated from my Queens, New York, apartment as we dissected what seemed like a nest of corruption drawn from the Borgia popes of the Renaissance. Except that now this was unfolding in the age of social media. Nothing could be hidden anymore. And at the center of the backstabbing, the cover-ups, and the underlying story of sexual abuse and harassment were bishops.

It was one thing for those of us in the limited circle of Catholic journalism. We knew the buzz, were not surprised by the Pennsylvania report findings, had perhaps grown numb after decades of exposure to the issue. But the impact was felt particularly among loyal in-the-pews Catholics who had presumed that all this was put aside after the revelations from the Boston Archdiocese, which led to the 2002 mandate from the U.S. bishops that all such cases should be reported and that priests found responsible would be taken out of ministry.

Much of that had happened. But the summer of 2018 brought it all back, in a different permutation. Around this time, I had a conversation with a Long Island grandmother and long-time Catholic. She said she would never go to Mass again. She could count a number of her friends who felt the same way. They were among the many loyal Catholics who felt their loyalty had been abused. The church hierarchy had obviously failed to police its own.

And so, again, why bother writing a book about a Catholic bishop?

The simple answer is that Thomas Gumbleton, auxiliary bishop of Detroit, is different. That uniqueness may hold a clue to what is possible in a renewed church. Such renewal would have to entail a transformation among the hierarchy. The medieval aura surrounding an all-knowing cleric was not going to fly in a social media age. Gumbleton's example could prove to be a model, even if—or particularly insofar as—he has for much of his career been a source of exasperation for his fellow bishops.

For me, this became a subject of focus in 2017 when I was assigned by the *National Catholic Reporter* to write Gumbleton's obituary. Though he was eighty-seven, the bishop was still very much alive at this point, and a call to his secretary about my project set off alarms. Nevertheless, it is a common practice among newspapers to prepare for the inevitable demise of famous people. The *National Catholic Reporter* wanted to be ready for Gumbleton's passing, whenever that might occur.

Most *NCR* readers hoped that would remain a distant event. Gumbleton may well be the quintessential *NCR* bishop. Founded in 1964 by visionary editor Robert Hoyt, the *National Catholic Reporter* grew out of Vatican II. The church was undergoing massive changes at the time, and there seemed to be no limit to the progressive reordering of a seemingly hidebound institution. The Mass became more inclusive and, with the use of the vernacular, more accessible. At the same time, the social dimension of the gospel was strongly emphasized. In civil rights marches of that era, it became common to find priests and nuns on the front lines. That was no accident. There was a heady spirit in the air. That aura of church involvement in social issues expanded to the rights of the laity in general, with faint hints of new movements on behalf of women and sexual minorities. The church was suddenly open and ready to listen. That was the spirit of the time.

And the *National Catholic Reporter*, growing out of a diocesan newspaper with wider ambitions to report on the church and the world, was in the forefront of chronicling these developments. Its readers were imbued with that spirit, either actively so or, in the pursuit of busy lives, at least wanting to know what was going on from the sidelines. They were a loyal bunch, with subscription renewals that routinely continued over decades. Among these readers, many of them came to have a special affection for the auxiliary bishop from Detroit.

As part of the obituary assignment, I poured over the extensive *NCR* files on Gumbleton. He was involved in seemingly everything of importance, often extending his activism well beyond parochial barriers. He was outside the main centers of power in the church, yet apparently inside of everything that really mattered.

I discovered a bishop who cropped up in every international hotspot: In Saigon, during the Vietnam War, protesting on behalf of political prisoners; in El Salvador, praying in the midst of a standoff between refugees and the military; in Iran, offering Christmas Mass for U.S. hostages, and upon his return encountering suspicion from the U.S. State Department; in his native Detroit, protesting his own archbishop's plans to close parishes; and at the Ohio state legislature, arguing for an end to the statute of limitations on sex abuse cases, a position stridently opposed by his fellow bishops.

He was also willing to take the entire structure of the hierarchy to task. Frequently he commented that those seeking an improvement in the quality of bishops were stymied by the system. Bishops were largely selected as auxiliaries to serve other bishops in dioceses. Those who made the appointments tended to be career men who had become comfortable in the corridors of church bureaucracy. They rarely wanted to be outshone; they would rarely select men who were brighter than or different from themselves. Gumbleton, as a bishop himself, was ensconced into the system, but he was willing to analyze its flaws—even, some would say, in a caustic manner.

Upon receiving an award in 2007 from Voice of the Faithful, a church reform group, Gumbleton said the key test for a bishop remained loyalty. "So you begin to get a structure where everything comes from the top and works its way down, so you don't get people who have initiative, who have imagination, who are creative, who are the type of people you need as leader. Leaders are not people who simply conform to what somebody else tells them," he said.[1]

Certainly Gumbleton was never ready simply to conform. He could never be labeled as a go-along-to-get-along type of leader. He was always out there, ready to challenge the church and the wider society on a wide array of fronts. In the heady days soon after Vatican II, that spirit was valued in church

---

1. Joe Feuerherd, "Gumbleton Decries Lack of Leaders," *National Catholic Reporter*, March 16, 2007.

circles, even by Gumbleton's boss, Cardinal John Dearden, who surely must have had to bite his tongue on occasion when his auxiliary staked out positions on a wide array of topics. And even as the church began to retreat from the spirit of renewal, Gumbleton never stopped, even into his eighties.

If anything, as he got older, his activism only got broader. He moved from civil rights and pacifism, where it was easier to draw clear support for his stances from church documents, into more hazy, and controversial spheres. While the church universal, during the papacies of John Paul II and Benedict XVI, underwent a general retrenchment, Gumbleton could be heard and seen offering consolation to advocates of women's ordination and gay rights, speaking to Catholics who remained in the pews yet sometimes felt estranged from their own local leaders.

This book is not a comprehensive biography. It is compiled from archives, particularly those of the *National Catholic Reporter*, and a series of three extensive interviews I conducted with the bishop over a year beginning in December 2017. He was extremely cooperative, with each session lasting for at least five hours. I would raise questions, and Bishop Gumbleton would provide remembrances, sometimes till we both would begin to feel the pangs of exhaustion (the octogenarian bishop regularly outpacing my energy). Later interviews with others who also lived through Gumbleton's times helped to fill in some gaps. These pages are, I hope, a glimpse into a remarkable life, sometimes highly publicized yet often shrouded in mystery about the motivations and thoughts of its central character.

But there remains another, more personal, reason to explore the life of this unusual bishop.

The Catholicism where I grew up at St. Anne's Parish in Garden City, Long Island, was marked by novenas, parish mission preachers, guitar Masses after Vatican II, and CYO football and basketball.

My father was a voracious reader and he subscribed, at various times, to a wildly divergent array of Catholic publications, including *Commonweal, America,* and the arch-conservative *Wanderer.* I would say he was not overly pietistic, although he did go to Mass every week. My mother was a spiritual explorer, ready to experience charismatic and healing Masses. My father preferred a quiet Sunday morning Mass with sedate music and a time set aside to get on his knees. But he was adventurous in his own way. He read most of the Catholic publications that came to our household, looking in particular for those dealing with contemporary issues. Proudly, he brought us to the public library in our town and had us seek out a piece he wrote for *America,* the Jesuit journal, on business and civil rights in the early 1960s.

He was, in retrospect, a rarity. Relatively few Catholics get caught up in the traditionalist/progressive church arguments. Catholic life, for most, is lived out in parishes, often far removed from overt political and social arguments.

But that was not the lesson I learned. Regardless of where one lay across the ideological spectrum, the message I heard was clear: Catholicism had a political and social dimension, reiterated in the papal social encyclicals, that could be debated and argued at length, even if the homily at Sunday Mass was often a kind of neutral series of pleasantries intended not to disturb a suburban Catholic audience.

What was intriguing about Catholicism, in my eyes, was how both progressives and traditionalists could scour its teachings and plausibly come up with their own way to apply it in the wider world. The Catholic emphasis on communal obligations to both family and the poor, subjects largely ignored in an increasingly American libertarian world, just seemed to make sense to me. Many of my generation—I am now in my sixties—moved on from active church life. That is even more the case among younger generations, particularly in the fallout from the sex abuse crisis. The Catholic Church is an admittedly hard sell, even more so today. But I've never left, even while immersed in the disheartening church scandals. I'm a true lifer. There really isn't a lot else out there with an all-encompassing humanistic and spiritual vision, at least when the tradition is acting at its best. In his own way, Gumbleton remains an embodiment of the tradition of Catholic social teaching active in the world, and as such is a figure worth paying attention to.

Another factor in my view of the church growing up was the far-away war in Southeast Asia, which frayed the informal alliance between the church and the patriotism of the World War II generation. At our parish school, I knew that a number of young male teachers were finding a respite from the draft in teaching catechism and history to suburban Long Island youth. They would often tell us about their own distress at what was happening in Southeast Asia. A nun, whom every male student had a crush on, showed us antiwar documentaries, thus upsetting some of the more conservative parents. Rumor had it that she hung out with the Berrigans and their friends, the types who were burning draft records.

My father, a World War II veteran and a fervent anti-Communist, was deeply troubled by what was going on with the emerging antiwar sentiment among many young Catholics. Dinner-time discussions often focused on the news of the day, which was generally terrible, as the war continued to rage and young men were sent off to a war they couldn't comprehend. I aged on the young side of that Vietnam generation curve. By the time I reached draft age, there was a volunteer army and the war, at least for Americans, was winding down, though the same could not be said for the Vietnamese left in its wake. With that background, I entered the less-than-lucrative but always fascinating field of Catholic journalism. In that realm Gumbleton was always popping up in stories, even as he was largely sidelined by his brother bishops. Eventually the war ended, and memories of Vietnam faded. Yet Gumbleton carried on the good fight, struggling against what he viewed as the tentacles of American empire extending from Central America to the Middle East.

In the early 1980s, I spent a year working in Detroit, where I would hear regular stories of chancery types railing against an auxiliary bishop with the audacity to take on the archbishop on various issues, including the closing of inner-city parishes. He also had his defenders. Those who opposed Cardinal Edmund Szoka's massive closing of Detroit city parishes found an ally in his auxiliary bishop. Gumbleton quietly, and sometimes not so quietly, rallied Detroit Catholics to the cause of small, urban parishes serving those living on the edge in a difficult city at a difficult time.

When I was unceremoniously dismissed from my job at the diocesan newspaper over a management dispute, Gumbleton offered a listening and sympathetic ear, even if he was far removed at that point from any direct power to provide assistance.

There he was: a part of the church hierarchy, yet willing to be critical of it at the same time. That balancing act would characterize his career over a period of fifty years as a bishop and before that as a priest. That balancing act, with all the tension and promise that it reflects, may point us in the direction of a future church that may arise from the ashes of the present season of scandal and disaffection. Named a bishop at the age of thirty-eight, Gumbleton's career, in earthly terms, largely stagnated. Once an up-and-coming chancery official in what was considered a model Vatican II archdiocese, Gumbleton never received a promotion. In a hierarchy filled with clerics aching for another step up the ladder—Theodore McCarrick's career from priest in New York to New Jersey bishop, to Vatican fundraiser, to Washington, DC, cardinal, is a cautionary illustration—Gumbleton early on decided he wasn't likely to move up. He had alienated too many people along the way. If he ever had qualms about this, they largely receded. His activism was not considered bishoplike, and, as John Paul II began enforcing a model for bishops who stuck to a mold of unwavering obedience, Gumbleton's work in Central America and his questioning of church teaching on issues such as women's ordination, assured that he would never be appointed to preside over his own diocese.

Paradoxically, the fact that Gumbleton never moved up made him, in many ways, more powerful. His independence from the need to placate superiors and the conservative money crowd allowed him to become a free agent. He wasn't leaving Detroit. That left him with time and energy to become a voice for those left behind in a church increasingly wrapped up in itself.

As the years moved on, the U.S. bishops stopped putting out pastoral statements on wide public issues such as their letters on the economy and the arms race, the latter, a document that Gumbleton helped to shape. Their meetings were focused on more parochial issues, and over time on such issues as abortion and religious freedom.

As the bishops moved on, Gumbleton in many ways stayed on the same path he had forged in the late 1960s. As a shepherd in the church who would always remain an auxiliary bishop, there was little to hold him back. Some of his friends said the tension created a more prophetic and dynamic Christian leader, freed from the restraints that a bishop's office usually imposes. Those who were less supportive frequently saw him as marginalized, fixated on concerns and causes that were now firmly ensconced in the rear-view mirror of mainstream Catholic life. Gumbleton, up into his late eighties, never went quietly. He continued to embrace that marginalized existence, seeing it as the fulfillment of the gospel. Jesus came to bring good news to the poor, and, as an auxiliary bishop, Gumbleton could always find opportunities to do the same.

Chapter 2

A Step Too Far

> *"He will impress many sitting in the pews with his profile in courage."*

On the feast of the Immaculate Conception, December 8, 2017, Bishop Thomas Gumbleton drove in his unfashionably bright red Toyota Camry to his office adjacent to St. Leo's Church, off Grand River in Detroit.

Gumbleton was a month shy of his eighty-eighth birthday. He walked rapidly, though with a slight hunch, through the morning cold. He was five-foot-eight-inches tall, an athletically trim 175 pounds, not too far from where he was at ordination in 1956. At that time, his brother had made him a bet that, like many newly ordained priests, well-fed by diligent rectory housekeepers, he would eventually put on weight. The young priest would win that bet. Now, six decades later, a shock of hair still hung over his forehead, much as it did when he first abandoned the clean-cut look he had fashioned as a seminarian and young priest in the 1950s and early '60s.

Gumbleton reached his bare office, which contained an office supply desk, a chair, a computer, and an old, lumpy couch. The office was most notable for what it lacked: no photos of family, much less pictures of himself shaking hands with popes, politicians, or business bigwigs. Not even historic pictures of his

Credit: Courtesy Thomas Gumbleton

own activism from the 1960s civil rights and Vietnam protests. Gumbleton's office stood adjacent to St. Leo's, a now-closed yet once-resplendent church. It was situated on a road that officially retained the title of boulevard, yet remained largely an unseemly mix of abandoned factories, low-rent houses, and bungalows. It also contained wide swaths of open space. Parts of urban Detroit offered surprising vistas of prairie grass, more reminiscent of rural Kansas than the hard-scrabble home of Motown.

Outside his office could be seen the small growing artist colonies of simple Quonset huts, with their modern art displayed out front, a sign of hope and revival. Gumbleton can recite the comings and goings of the neighborhood with the ease of an old-time resident, which is what he is. St. Leo's had been sold by the archdiocese, and it would soon be reopened as a gospel-choir venue, perhaps reinvigorating the boulevard's nascent cultural scene.

St. Leo's and Gumbleton were once intertwined. He took over the parish in 1983, years after it had fallen in a precipitous decline with the rest of the city. In many ways the city still is recovering from the events of 1967, which police officers and reporters routinely refer to as the riots, but which many activists remember as "the insurrection." That issue of vocabulary regarding events that left forty-three people dead and caused the destruction of wide swaths of the city is just an example of the divisions that have marked Detroit life ever since.

From the time he arrived, Gumbleton worked to rebuild trust, not an easy task for a white cleric in a neighborhood where blacks had once been discouraged from attending St. Leo's and advised to attend their "own church." Soon after 1967, those white naysayers themselves began departing for the suburbs. In the years after his arrival, no matter where his travels might take him, Gumbleton always made a point of returning to the small parish every Sunday. There he preached an unvarnished gospel, free of the caveats and the restraints imposed by better-off congregations uncomfortable with a radical, social justice-driven Jesus. Though his preaching style remained soft spoken, his words sometimes contained an element of what his critics would term wrath but his friends would call prophetic.

When that prophetic voice focused on the shortcomings of the world outside the church, Gumbleton could be tolerated, even by those clerics who disagreed with him. Critiquing U.S. policy toward Iran or Central America might raise the hackles of more conservative types, but Gumbleton was largely on the firm ground of Catholic social teaching, even if his calls for nonviolence were dismissed as quixotic. But when he took on the sins of the church, Gumbleton found little welcome among most of his brother bishops. After years of continued prophetic utterances, the auxiliary bishop had gone too far.

In 2007, Gumbleton was told by his then-boss, Cardinal Adam Maida, that he could no longer minister in the parish. He was given a week to pack up his things. He collected his few belongings and moved into a downtown apartment. It was clear that he was being banished, even if the official line from the archdiocese was that this was simply a routine personnel matter. It wasn't.[1]

In the world of Catholic bishops, there is a tradition of collegiality and mutual support, at least in public statements. Even if bishops cannot stand each other in private, in public they are prone to seek cohesion and unity. But it seems that Gumbleton had crossed a line that demanded his expulsion. The issue was sex abuse. And in the big picture, Gumbleton had touched the third rail of ecclesial politics.

It was just five years after the revelations in the *Boston Globe* shined a spotlight on Cardinal Bernard Law's handling of cases of priestly sex abuse in Boston. The conservative archbishop, perhaps the most powerful figure in the church hierarchy at the time, had allowed scores of priests credibly accused of sex abuse to be moved from parish to parish, where they continued to prey on young children.

After years of stonewalling, the *Globe* revelations sparked a furor, both inside and outside the church. They came nearly twenty years after an *NCR* series on notorious sex abuse cases in the Diocese of Lafayette, Louisiana, had broken the lid off the subject. In the intervening twenty years, there was a steady drip of new revelations. But the Boston cases, which numbered in the hundreds, caught national attention, thanks to the *Globe's* prominence in media circles.

More cases became apparent around the country and, later, in the world. It was clear that Boston was not just a quirk. The outcry caused Law to resign, and he spent his retirement years in a Roman basilica, where he was accorded full dignity and respect, seemingly as if nothing had ever cast a cloud on his leadership. Upon his death during the 2017 Christmas season, he was remembered almost solely for his involvement in the sex abuse cover-up. Nevertheless, Pope Francis attended his funeral, a fact protested by sex abuse survivors who argued that Law did not deserve high honors.

---

1. Laurie Goodstein, "Outspoken Catholic Pastor Replaced; He Says It's Retaliation," *New York Times*, June 26, 2007, A 14.

Just five years after the *Boston Globe* revelations, later dramatized in *Spotlight*, an Oscar-winning film, the U.S. bishops were still under siege. They had implemented norms established at a 2002 meeting of the bishops in Dallas, mandating a zero-tolerance policy on priestly sex abuse. Those credibly accused of sex abuse were told they were no longer welcome to minister, an acknowledgment that public dissatisfaction had reached a crescendo that was finally being heard.

Still, new revelations from around the country continued. To be fair, many of the issues revolved around older cases, where bishops had shuffled sex abusers around to treatment centers and other parishes and dioceses where they could start anew, sometimes beginning an entirely new round of abuse on unsuspecting parishioners.

District attorneys on Long Island and in Philadelphia convened grand juries that detailed horrific tales of sex abuse in parishes that bishops had, on the whole, either ignored or, after being informed, dealt with by moving priests around. The bishops were clearly overwhelmed by the evidence that they had ignored horrific wrongdoing, hoping that therapy and new pastoral settings would change the behavior of abusive priests. Often it didn't. Rare was a diocese left untouched by the scandal, as hundreds of victims came forward, often in poignant public demonstrations. One group, Survivors Network of those Abused by Priests (SNAP), were fixtures outside chancery offices. They were comprised of sex abuse survivors. Their signature tactic was to present pictures of themselves as children, a reminder of how predators had taken advantage of the innocent.

The church faced a crisis that some compared in its magnitude to the Reformation. Church attendance declined, particularly in New England, where the primary focus on the crisis landed. Those Catholics who remained in the pews called for action. Some formed organizations like Voice of the Faithful, which took upon itself the task of monitoring bishops to assure that they were following the dictates of the Dallas Charter. A rupture in trust existed between the laity and their leaders.

Few doubted the veracity of most of the claims. But because of statutes of limitations, the vast majority of these cases were beyond the reach of the law. In most cases, public officials could only issue damning reports. Amidst this outcry, the public pressure to do something began to exert itself. Politicians were beginning to hear from their constituents. Scores of state houses were considering remedies, bringing the political process to bear on what had previously been perceived as an internal church matter.

State legislatures began passing bills that would extend the statute of limitations in such cases. The crimes often occurred when the victims were children, and their inability to process what happened to them, largely out of fear and shaming, allowed legal time limits to pass by. Already California had opened a window, allowing victims to sue the church; the ongoing revelations resulted in the disgrace of more than one prominent churchman, including Cardinal Roger Mahony of Los Angeles.

Other dioceses were either threatened with or had succumbed to bankruptcy as the pain of massive settlements drained diocesan coffers. Among them was the Diocese of Wilmington, Delaware, which was forced into bankruptcy after the state legislature extended the statute of limitations.

In response, across the nation, bishops went to state capitals, from Denver to Albany, pleading with legislators that the church had cleaned up its act, that there were few new cases of sex abuse being reported, and that the church had established an elaborate system of security checks so that sex abusers could no longer have unfettered access to children. If the statute of limitations were extended, state legislators were warned, the burden of old cases would bring an end to Catholic charitable and educational functions in their states.

While church leaders continued to press their agenda on a host of other topics, including the right to life and support for the poor and immigrants, the issue of statutes of limitations remained a top priority for the bishops. Regularly their lobbying efforts were countered by groups like SNAP, whose dramatic demonstrations captured the public imagination in a way that the bishops' lobbying efforts could never match. But the bishops countered in their own way. Catholic legislators who voted to extend the statute of limitations found themselves singled out and threatened with organized voting campaigns. Into the middle of this storm strode Gumbleton. He had struck up a long-standing friendship with SNAP leader and founder Barbara Blaine. Gumbleton was convinced that his fellow bishops were wrong on this point and that his friend Blaine, who had been abused while a girl in a Toledo, Ohio, parish, was right. Victims, he said, deserved their day in court, even regarding events that had occurred decades before and might prove difficult to reconstruct as memories faded and participants died.

"I am not out to get the Ohio bishops, but I care about these victims. I have a deep sense of compassion for how difficult it has been for them," he told *USA Today* at the time. Press coverage was largely positive. That made Gumbleton's problems with his fellow bishops even more dramatic.[2]

The *Toledo Blade* praised him. He "may not win friends and influence people in high places in the Roman Catholic Church, but he will impress many sitting in the pews with his profile in courage," the paper opined.[3]

Blaine was part of a large, devout Catholic family raised in Toledo. Her nightmare of abuse began in 1969, when she was a thirteen-year-old at St. Pius X School. Her abuser would later be named in multiple sex abuse lawsuits. Even with her horrific experience, Blaine, who died suddenly in 2017 at the age of sixty-one, remained a faithful Catholic who had devoted much of her life to the causes dear to Gumbleton's heart. She had lived in a Catholic Worker house in Chicago and volunteered for Pax Christi, the Catholic peace organization, when

2. Cathy Lynn Grossman, "Bishop Declares He Was Abused," *USA Today*, January 12, 2006, D10.

3. "The Bishop as Victim," *Toledo Blade*, January 19, 2006, A10.

Gumbleton had held a leadership role. She had started SNAP after reading a series in the *National Catholic Reporter* about sex abusers written by Jason Berry. In subsequent years, she had become a public nudge for the bishops. Her work on sex abuse by priests became a full-time job after the *Boston Globe* revelations in 2002, when the organization was besieged with phone calls from survivors.

Quoted in the *National Catholic Reporter* after her death, Gumbleton noted that Blaine's influence inspired his own views in coming out against many of his fellow bishops, who were still reluctant to embrace survivors for fear that this would result in more lawsuits directed against the church.

"I had bishops tell me she was practically a devil against the church," recalled Gumbleton. But, he said, "SNAP was one of the most important things that happened in bringing the sex abuse crisis to the forefront, and it caused the bishops to do much more than they were doing, and it helped stop the cover-up."[4]

At the time, legislators were considering a bill that would extend the statute of limitations in Blaine's native Ohio. SNAP saw the possibility of picking off a key Midwestern and strongly Catholic state. The movement was cascading, having already made inroads in California; and it was moving toward the middle of the country.

Toledo is only an hour's drive from Detroit, and Gumbleton personally knew the then-bishop, James Robert Hoffman. He pled Blaine's case to the bishop and got nowhere. Hoffman and his fellow Ohio bishops were adamant: the church could not afford to lose the statute of limitations protection in the state. Any changes in that regard would bankrupt the state's dioceses, they argued. The entire network of parishes and Catholic Charities was under siege with this proposed legislation, they said.

---

4. Bishop Gumbleton, interview with author, December 2017.

Still, Blaine asked Gumbleton to testify at the state house for the proposed bill. He agreed. Without warning to his fellow bishops, either in Michigan or Ohio, Gumbleton made the three-and-a half-hour drive down to Columbus for a hearing. It was typical Gumbleton style. Soft-spoken, almost to a fault, but with a damn-the-torpedoes attitude when others might have shied away.

"I never thought of the consequences," he admitted in an interview a decade later. "I wasn't on any track [up the church hierarchy]. In some ways I should have been more cautious. But I had a responsibility to say what I knew. I thought it was the right thing to do."[5]

It was more than a public discussion of a policy issue in front of one state legislature. Gumbleton brought a personal dynamic to the issue. During his testimony, Gumbleton revealed that he had been accosted while in junior seminary by a priest teacher. He was fifteen at the time. It was the first time he had talked to anyone about the abuse, which had taken place more than five decades before.

At the time, he had wondered if he was the only one. As was usual in these cases, the answer was that he was not alone. The priest in question, by now long dead, was well known among the seminary boys at the time, even if they didn't talk about it openly. His classmates, both those who were ordained and those who weren't, confirmed his story, noting that the priest in question had also approached them.

"I pushed the guy away," Gumbleton later recalled, noting that the predator never actually got very far with him. The priest brought him and his fellow Sacred Heart Seminary students for overnight visits to a cottage. Part of the visit included wrestling matches, and the priest put his hand down the pants of young Gumbleton. His own silence over the decades gave Gumbleton insight into the shame and guilt that many survivors felt, partic-

5. Ibid.

ularly those who experienced abuse in a Catholic setting where God and faith mixed with a toxic brew of exploitation.

He downplayed its implications on his own personal development. "It was not that I was victimized in a way that I was totally traumatized," he told the *Toledo Blade,* after his Ohio legislative testimony. "At 15, I was still very young, naïve and immature. I did not fully understand what was going on," he said. But he felt obligated to tell his story at that hearing at a time when the curse of sex abuse was coming more into the light of day.[6]

He told *USA Today*: "It might seem easier to keep the evils hidden, to move on and trust that the future will be better. But I am convinced that a settlement of every case by our court system is the only way to protect children and to heal the brokenness with the church."[7]

Gumbleton was the first U.S. bishop to acknowledge that he himself had been a victim of a priest abuser. The little hearing in the Ohio statehouse created worldwide repercussions. Gumbleton spent some five hours that day in interviews with reporters, including those from Ohio, Michigan, and nationally. His testimony generated newspaper and television headlines. There was a cost to being so public. Bill O'Brien, a Detroit community organizer and friend of Gumbleton, shared breakfast with him the next morning. He could tell the auxiliary bishop was worried. He had a right to be.[8]

After the testimony made headlines, the bishops of Ohio contacted the papal nuncio who told Gumbleton he was being retired as auxiliary bishop and as pastor of St. Leo's. Within a week, he had been evicted from his rectory and moved into a downtown Detroit apartment, where he was to live out the rest of his days. It was a move of just a few miles, but the message was clear. Gumbleton was exiled.

---

6. Jim Provance, "Detroit Bishop Backs Retroactive Suits," *Toledo Blade,* January 12, 2006.

7. Grossman, "Bishop Declares He Was Abused," D10.

8. Bill O'Brien, phone interview with author, December 2018.

It was a loss for both the bishop and for the people of St. Leo's. "The people loved him and he loved them," said his nephew, Gerry Gumbleton. Yet, "he was a man of principle. In his mind, this was something he had to do. But it cost him." Looking back a decade later, Bishop Gumbleton tried to be philosophical.[9] He felt that the bishops had made scores of mistakes in handling the sex abuse crisis. Still he didn't view them as evil or horribly incompetent. It was because they had abdicated their pastoral responsibilities, he would say. Instead of seeing the thousands of victims, such as Blaine, as a part of their flock who needed healing and response, victims were seen primarily as potential legal cases. The bishops first listened to their lawyers, whose main goal was to limit liability. The pattern repeated itself across the country, from Law's Boston to Mahony's Los Angeles. The bishops argued that the church was being unfairly singled out. The bishops' defenders would point to public schools, for instance, where there was reason to believe that sex abuse was a continuing problem, but which most statute of limitations legislation would exempt.

Gumbleton countered that the church had to clean its own house, and that it had made tragic mistakes in handing the crisis over to its lawyers and state house lobbyists.

"How terrible is that? We have to get rid of this idea that we go into court. A courtroom in our law system is adversarial. The people on the other side are your enemy. We have to beat them in court. We have to give up that notion. Bishops should be pastors, shepherds, people who love their whole flock and work for the good of the flock," he said about the crisis in 2018, in the midst of a summer that had seen scandal blow up once again.[10]

From his own experience, he knew that victims, especially those who were attacked at a young age, take years to come to grips with their assaults. In his case, it had taken nearly six

9. Bishop Gumbleton, interview with author, December 2017.

10. Thomas Gumbleton, "During Abuse Crisis, Follow Jesus to Bring Change to Church," *National Catholic Reporter*, August 30, 2018.

decades. That was reason enough to want to rid these cases of the statutes of limitations, Gumbleton thought. It was the reason he went to Ohio.

But Gumbleton's trip to Ohio wasn't a spur-of-the-moment event. It was the culmination of a long, ongoing process. He had made a point of visiting with the families of victims who were refused audiences by other bishops. In one family in the neighboring Diocese of Lansing, Gumbleton befriended a family with two sons who had been abused by a priest. One of those sons later committed suicide. The local bishop had refused to see them.

Gumbleton argued that his fellow bishops were wrong. But he added more than just a legal and political argument. He viewed it as a moral and religious obligation to stand up for the most vulnerable. But he knew that some of his fellow bishops would be displeased. He was right about that.

While the archdiocese tried to spin the event of his transfer from St. Leo's as a routine move for a bishop past the age of retirement, Gumbleton, in typical style, would have none of that.

"I did not choose to leave St. Leo's," he told the *New York Times*. "It's something that was forced upon me." The *Times* interviewed three canon lawyers, who agreed that there was nothing in canon law prohibiting Maida from keeping Gumbleton right where he was. His move from St. Leo's, away from the room where he resided in back of the church, was greeted with sorrow and bewilderment by the small congregation.

"Everyone in the parish is hurt and angry," said Mary M. Black, a parishioner quoted by the *Times*. St. Leo's was his home. And it was home, as well, for those parishioners who had grown to love him.

Black noted how incredibly accessible the bishop was to the people of the parish.

"He talks after Mass with people, and he is there ahead of Mass to say the Rosary for anybody who has problems. And we all have his personal phone number. You do not have to go through a secretary. He was a pastor in the truest sense of the word," she told the *Times*.[11]

Still, despite the protestations, Gumbleton was gone from his parish. He would never return as pastor.

If Bishop Gumbleton had finally crossed an unforgiveable line, it was not the first time he had tested the limits of proper bishop behavior. This unusually soft-spoken, quiet, and introverted cleric had long been a rebel whose causes rubbed against the expectations of what many considered his job. He had long been formally left to languish as an auxiliary bishop. Now that had been taken away from him, in reality if not in actual title. For Gumbleton's critics, it had been a long time coming. Even his friends had expected this kind of reaction. In an institution that values smooth sailing, Gumbleton had been a notorious and long-time rocker of boats. His trip to Ohio had not been out of character.

---

11. Goodstein, "Outspoken Catholic Pastor Replaced," A 14.

Chapter 3

Motown Product

"If you hit him, you could expect to be hit back."

A Toyota was perhaps the only non-Detroit attribute Gumbleton possessed.

Driving up Grand River Boulevard in his eighty-eighth year in the early summer of 2018, he lamented how what was once a solid Catholic community had been transformed over the years. A neighborhood once dotted with stores, including a butcher shop where patrons were treated to the wringing of the neck of the bird they were to purchase, was, by the 1990s, a patchwork of empty lots, churches, liquor stores, and a smattering of African American Pentecostal churches, often occupying the shells of former Catholic parishes.

Gumbleton remembered when there was a roster of active parishes, including St. Teresa's nearby and, around the corner, Epiphany, where a young Gumbleton would accompany his father at weekday Mass at 6 a.m. before heading, respectively, to school or to work. Except for short stints as a graduate student in Rome and in St. John's Seminary out in Plymouth, Michigan, Gumbleton would never live beyond a ten-mile arc from where he grew up in east Detroit on Manor Street.

On that June day in 2018, the old house on Manor Street was a bungalow overrun with weeds. Some of the homes nearby are well kept by long-time residents and newcomers. But others lie abandoned. If his family's former house has an owner living there, it is not apparent on a drive through on a quiet late spring morning.

Thomas John Gumbleton was born in that old bungalow on January 26, 1930. He was number six of what would eventually blossom into an Irish Catholic American Midwest family featuring nine children.

There wasn't a lot of space in the Gumbleton household. The children shared a single room, with one bed relegated to oldest brother Vincent; another for brothers Gerard, Raymond, John, James, Daniel, and Tom; and another for sisters Loretta and Irene.

His early years were spent during the hardscrabble years of the Great Depression, but by the time young Gumbleton reached the age where he could figure out some idea of what was going on around him, Detroit was experiencing a boom. As the city emerged from labor strife and the massive unemployment of the Depression, it quickly bustled with industry as the national economy geared up for war. The region rapidly reached full employment. There was a need for workers, matched by a great migration of African Americans from the South. Factories that had been designed for automobiles were soon churning out tanks and planes.

In 1943, while the world was engulfed in war, thirteen-year-old Tom Gumbleton would take the trolley down Grand River and then connect to Tiger Stadium, where he worked as an usher. With most of the team's players swept up in the war effort, the Tigers posted a 78-76 record and landed in fifth place, twenty games behind the winning New York Yankees. They attracted a total of 600,000 paying spectators, a little more than 8,000 per game.[1]

A young Gumbleton would escort patrons to their seats and, for a dime or a fifteen-cent tip, would clean the dust from the chairs. He loved the work. "I got into every ballgame for free," he recalled decades later. In 1943, he would earn a dollar and

1. 1943 Detroit Tigers statistics, Baseball-reference.com.

sometimes up to a $1.50 per game, good money for a thirteen-year-old Detroiter in those days.

For Gumbleton, the East Detroit neighborhood was a place for growth and excitement. At the local public high school, he learned to swim. One block over was Epiphany Church. The family knew they could get to Mass in five minutes, door-to door. They had it all timed. Thoughts about becoming a priest reverberated in his head as a fourth grader, as they did for many Catholic young men of his generation. His older brother Gerry had gone off to seminary high school. As a result, young Tom had learned to enjoy tagging along, hanging out at Sacred Heart Seminary, over by Chicago Boulevard, at the time a bustling enclave filled with adolescent male energy, as well as a heavy dose of traditional Catholic piety.

But thoughts of seminary remained just a part of a busy life. Over on Plymouth and Grand River was an athletic supply store. There he would watch television, then a new invention that had not yet arrived in his home, and he became enthralled by hockey, particularly games played by the Detroit Red Wings over at nearby Olympia Stadium. Athletics would always play a role in Gumbleton's life. While in seminary, and even through the early years of priesthood, he became known as an aggressive hockey and basketball player. Into his eighties, he would attend Red Wings hockey and Tigers games, sometimes with season tickets offered by family friends.

Gumbleton may have emerged as the most pacifistic American bishop, but he was also known as a fierce competitor. An *NCR* profile of Gumbleton in 1990 by Arthur Jones describes Gumbleton as a man driven by athletic competition. As a young priest, he was part of a hockey club comprised of his fellow Detroit clergy. They would play against police offiers or fellow clergy from Ontario. They would put down $20 to rent a rink every Thursday night. One night Gumbleton, the team's left-winger (in stark hockey terms if not in politics), suffered a blow to the head from a puck. Though he was bleeding profusely, it took a while for his fellow priests to get him to the hospital;

they only had an hour to play and didn't want to interrupt the competition.[2]

Bill Carry, a former New Yorker and friend, said that Gumbleton regularly rooted for the Yankees when he wasn't rooting for the Tigers. "It's because they know how to win," Gumbleton would say. Bill and his wife would take their bishop friend along on family camping trips. One time the group had a softball game. Gumbleton broke a rib while making a play at second base. He kept the pain and discomfort to himself; he didn't want to admit that the agony was caused by his collision with the couple's thirteen-year-old daughter.[3] Father Norman Thomas, the longtime pastor of Sacred Heart Church in Detroit, said his classmate was known for competitiveness, whether it was on the basketball court or the hockey rink. "If you hit him, you could expect to be hit back," said Thomas about his friend's hockey days.[4]

But the athletic life was to remain a sideline. The vocation of priesthood seemed to fit Gumbleton early on. Friends and family were not surprised about his embrace of the vocation and his ability to stick it out, even as many of his classmates over the years departed. "It was his calling. No doubt about it," Gerry Gumbleton, his nephew, would recall. Norman Thomas knew the future auxiliary bishop during an era when doctrines were settled and the church seemed an unchanging bulwark. "I don't recall any great theological discussion at the time," Norman Thomas said. "It wasn't till after Vatican II that there was a lot more talk and controversy."[5]

Seminary life in many ways offered a respite from many of the tensions growing up in an overcrowded house on Detroit's East Side. With such a large brood, there were bound to be issues. Gumbleton's sister Loretta, the firstborn in the family, was the product of a difficult breach birth, which resulted in

---

2. Arthur Jones, "Bishop Gumbleton, Combative Pacifist," *National Catholic Reporter,* November 16, 1990.
3. Bill and Mary Carry, phone interview with author, July 2017.
4. Norman Thomas, phone interview with author, 2017.
5. Ibid.

brain damage. As Tom's mother did not want her firstborn sent off to an institution, she lived with the rest of the family for most of her early years. Tom can remember watching his sister hit the ground, as she suffered regular fits and seizures. When caring for her finally proved too much for the family, Tom's parents were persuaded to place her in an institution in Lapeer, a sixty-mile drive from Detroit. Every month they would make the difficult trek back and forth, through local pre-interstate roads.

Meanwhile, thanks to trolleys and buses, Tom eagerly explored the neighborhood and the wider city of Detroit. Winters back then were typically harsh. The streets would cake up in snow and then ice over, offering the neighborhood kids their own skating rinks. In the summer, there was swimming off Belle Isle, the city's magnificent park in the middle of the Detroit River. In the winter, the channels around the island would freeze, creating an ice-skating wonderland. It was like being in the Netherlands, Gumbleton would later recall.

At home, his father, Vincent Gumbleton, was possessed of a particular kind of masculine Irish piety. It was a regular part of life. At night there were prayers before bedtime. In the morning, before work, young Tom would get up early to accompany his father to daily Mass.

Though the name was often taken for German, the Gumbletons were Irish; in fact, they could trace their history in Ireland for some five centuries. Pursuing the family history became something of a hobby for Tom's father. Decades later, at an international Pax Christi event in Northern Ireland, Gumbleton visited families with the same name—possibly long-lost cousins—and drank a few beers at a Gumbleton pub.

Vincent grew up in Holy Redeemer Parish. He worked right out of high school at a local manufacturing plant, where he could walk to work. His career was interrupted only by a short stint after being drafted for World War I, which mercifully concluded before he could be sent overseas.

At the parish, he met Helen Steintrager, who, after tenth grade, moved on to secretarial school. The details of their romance were not shared with their nine children. In any case, it must have been intense in its own way. They married in 1921, when he was twenty-one and she was nineteen.

Vincent was determined and ambitious. By 1932 he had graduated from college, completing credits in night school from the University of Detroit. By that time, the couple had already brought six children into the world, with Tom being the youngest. In 1954 the company where he worked was sold to Rockwell International, with most of its operations transferred to the home base in Pittsburgh. The family sweated the possibility that they would be forced to move from their beloved Detroit, but Vincent was able to convince his bosses to let him stay on in Michigan, where he eventually rose to the rather lofty position of vice president of purchasing.

While his dad pursued his business career, finally earning enough money to better support his large family, Tom entered Sacred Heart Seminary across town. Set amidst a series of imposing, monastic-style buildings, the seminary was located in the middle of an urban neighborhood, among Detroit's traditionally middle-class enclaves, not far from Blessed Sacrament Cathedral.

Tom recalls being attracted to the seminary because of his dream of being a priest, of course, but also because he liked the lifestyle. Classes and sports lasted throughout the day. The place provided an intimate enclave for a young adolescent boy in postwar Detroit.

Classes would go through the day, and students were expected to put in a half day of class time on Saturdays as well. (In retrospect, Tom wondered if that wasn't to keep the seminarians occupied throughout the dangerous temptations of weekends.)

It was a hermetically sealed world. Young Gumbleton reveled in the structure. High school seminaries at the time would feature Latin with doses of theology and other regular academic subjects. The classes for a bright boy like Tom were not overly challenging, but the all-male competition both in the classroom and on the playing fields resulted in life-long friendships that carried on to his eighties, both among those who went on to be ordained and those who left.

Tom was one of those who stayed on, both through junior seminary at Sacred Heart and then through St. John's major seminary out in Plymouth, located near a golf course said to be a favorite of Cardinal Edward Mooney, and later, after ordination, when many of his fellow classmates succumbed to the giant social upheavals that shook the church after Vatican II. The decision to leave seminary was a difficult one for many of his classmates. Those who left often carried a burden of failure or disgrace in the eyes of their pious families. Young Gumbleton didn't feel that kind of pressure. His parents made it clear that he always had their permission to leave. His older brother Gerry had done just that. Tom stayed because he liked it, not because he felt there was any stigma attached to leaving.

He took the bus and the trolley crosstown. Classes and activities would run into the night. There was so much to do that Tom sought his parents' permission to stay overnight at the seminary. His mother adamantly said no.

She gave no reason. Having broached the subject, Tom let it slide. He later would credit his mother with a wise decision. Though she never explained why, he thought that intuitively she knew that her boy's development would be aided by at least some time spent away from the hothouse atmosphere of seminary.[6]

But coming back to Manor Street meant interacting with a large family. That included his older sister Irene and her many friends. The two siblings were only thirteen months apart, so her friends were close enough in age to interact with. He grew accustomed to having women around, a point that later served him well as a celibate priest. To him, women were part of the scene, not foreign and frightening objects. A review of Thomas Merton's *Seven Storey Mountain*, written for a class at Sacred

6. Bishop Gumbleton, interview with author, June 2018.

Heart Seminary, reveals something of the thought of the young Gumbleton. There is a tone of youthful confidence and single-mindedness. Gumbleton embraced the famous monk's single-minded commitment to God.

That feeling held in his own seminary development. By the time ordination came in 1956, while still a youthful twenty-six, and after studies at the major seminary, St. John's in Plymouth, Michigan, Gumbleton had no doubts that this was the life he wanted. After all, he had been pursuing this goal since the ninth grade. Ordained by Cardinal Mooney at Blessed Sacrament Cathedral in Detroit, he was one of thirty archdiocesan priests ordained, along with twenty-one from other Michigan dioceses. This was, at the time, the second largest ordination class in the history of the archdiocese. Today, the yearly ordination schedule will include no more than a handful. At reunions for his ordination class, Gumbleton recounts ruefully, the number that left the active ministry to get married outnumbers those, like him, who stayed. Wives outnumber those who remain as active priests.

But he was confident in his vocation. The tension Gumbleton felt at the time was not existential or spiritual. He worried about his singing voice; tone deafness plagued him throughout his liturgical career. He trained for High Mass and listened to tapes incessantly. By doing so, by dint of sheer effort, Gumbleton discovered that he was able, if he started in the right place, to get through a sung Mass.

His first assignment was to St. Alphonsus Church in Dearborn, an inner Detroit suburb known for its huge Ford plant, the place where Henry Ford pioneered a new industrial revolution. At the time, the jobs were plentiful, the pay was good. And St. Alphonsus, with more than four thousand families, was thriving. Though largely a Polish parish, being in the suburbs, it was not officially considered an ethnic church (a designation usually confined to older churches in the city limits). There were benefits to being in Dearborn. When it snowed, the church parking lot and nearby streets were cleaned quickly, thanks to Ford Company taxes, which left the city flush with cash.

There was no shortage of priests at the time. If anything, there was an abundance of priests. Gumbleton served with three other associates as well as a pastor. (Today, most parishes in the United States have a single priest, the pastor, who is often absorbed in financial and administrative details, and whose ministerial skills are often directed toward organizing lay people and deacons to do the actual outreach.)

Sick calls were routine. Gumbleton, with his fellow curates, would have a list of up to twenty sick parishioners to visit regularly with the sacraments. The associates would rotate turns at night, ready to spring into action if the call came that a parishioner was dying and needed last rites.

A big part of the job was marriage preparation. Gumbleton felt ill-equipped to render advice. But in the heavily clerical atmosphere of the church of the time, that was not an impediment. "I don't know if I was competent to do it. I was a priest, and we were supposed to know everything," recalled Gumbleton. They were also expected to have insights for those in troubled marriages.

Up to fifty new converts could be expected each year at the parish, and it was up to the priests to prepare them for initiation into the church. Most were the spouses of Catholics, but there were also random people who would simply show up at the rectory door, interested in receiving instruction.

Once a thirteen-year-old girl showed up. Her name was Lynn. Neither of her parents was Catholic, but she wanted in. Gumbleton oversaw her instruction. This proved to be a long-term commitment. Following her baptism, Lynn went on to Catholic school, joined a religious order for a time, got married, had children, and is now the matriarch of four generations of Catholics. She stayed in touch with Gumbleton and regularly sought his spiritual advice.

"We did everything," said Gumbleton about his days in Dearborn. The pastor, Bishop Alexander M. Zaleski, then a Detroit auxiliary who later became bishop of Lansing, Michigan, operated in a way as to encourage creativity among his

Credit: Courtesy Thomas Gumbleton

young priests. The curates selected their own ministries. It was a creative time. Gumbleton became immersed in the entire project of the parish, working from sunup to bedtime.

He taught religious education, both to public school students and to students at the parish grade school and high school. (More than six decades later, those connections are still maintained.) And then there was Mass. On Sundays, liturgy was constant, with services at 5:30, 7:00, 8:45, 11:00 a.m., and 12:30 p.m., all to accommodate what was a burgeoning suburban 1950s American Catholic parish. To top it off, Gumbleton became a part of the men's bowling league, a chance to interact with parishioners on an informal level.

On Saturday nights, there were confessions. This might last for two and a half hours, during which he would hear confessions from as many as forty parishioners. "A lot of it was out of fear," recalled Gumbleton. Avoiding hell was the goal. Beneath the veneer of a bustling parish, there was an ugly side. Dearborn's leadership was notoriously racist, and the church had little to say about that. Much to his later regret, Gumbleton counts himself among those who were apathetic in the face of this massive social sin.

While Ford had long been open to black workers, Dearborn's long-time mayor Orville Hubbard (he served fifteen terms) pledged that no black people would ever be allowed to live in his city. He kept getting reelected on that pledge. According to his *New York Times* obituary, Hubbard became famous for ordering his police department to stand down as residents of a white neighborhood stoned a house that was being sold to a black family.[7]

"Nobody talked about it," Gumbleton said. "I never thought about how wrong that was. I never preached about it, I never thought about the sin of racism." Asked as he approached eighty-nine years of age if he had any regrets, that is what came to mind. It was those days at St. Alphonsus, when a clear social evil of racism reared its ugly head, and the then-Father Gumbleton simply kept his head down, ministering as a parish priest. It was a sin of omission he has long regretted. Reflecting back on that time, he says he recognized racist personal attitudes in people but didn't get the connection that a whole social structure, such as Dearborn at the time, could promote social sin.

His scathing critique of institutional sin would have to wait for another time. As a young priest, he was immersed in the details of parish life. It was a busy time. Peace and justice would have to wait.

---

7. Shawn G. Kennedy, "Orville L. Hubbard of Dearborn; Ex-Mayor a Foe of Integration," *New York Times*, December 17, 1982.

Chapter 4

The Catholic Case against the Vietnam War

"By the time the evening was over I was convinced they were right and that I should join their protest. I was changed."

Ordained in 1956 at the young age of twenty-six, Gumbleton was raised in a church structure that valued orderliness and, in the United States, allegiance to American values. In the Cold War struggle against Communism, the church and the nation's interests were seen as one.

Early on, Gumbleton was seen as a potential up-and-comer. After spending four years as an associate pastor at St. Alphonsus Parish in Dearborn, Michigan, Gumbleton was sent to Rome to study canon law. It was an indication that the young cleric was being tapped for bigger things. To study canon law in Rome meant that a priest was seen as potential chancery material.

Gumbleton arrived in the Eternal City at a critical juncture. Vatican II was underway, a massive meeting of the world's bishops, charged with renewing the church and fashioning a more open stance toward the modern world. For most Catholics, the most immediate changes took place in liturgy. No longer would the priest say Mass with his back to the people. The vernacular language—English in this case—replaced the traditional Latin. Now the congregation was expected to participate in the liturgy. Some priests took to the changes better than others.

Besides the changes in Sunday Mass, Vatican II introduced a new spirit of engagement with the secular world and issues of social justice. For the curate from Dearborn who had never thought that casual racism could be construed as a sin, the church's new energy provided a very different concept of church life. The council strongly deplored anti-Semitism and encouraged a new era of ecumenical dialogue with the Protestant world. The laity were encouraged to take up their rightful place as full members of the church, with a special role in shaping society along gospel principles.

In contrast to previous church councils, Vatican II issued no condemnations—with one exception. In the "Constitution on the Church in the Modern World" (*Gaudium et Spes*), the council fathers wrote: "Any act of war aimed indiscriminately at the destruction of entire cities or of extensive areas along with their population is a crime against God and man himself. It merits unequivocal and unhesitating condemnation" (no. 80.3). This statement would later have a decisive impact on the emerging consciousness of the then-young priest from Detroit.[1]

For most American Catholics, including the vast majority of priests, the events of Vatican II took place at a distance, its missives filtered via newspaper and magazine reports (The *New Yorker*, in particular, published extensive accounts of the proceedings). Apart from an occasional look at the pageantry featuring Pope John XXIII, television paid little attention to the proceedings. But among educated Catholics and many priests, there was a sense that something was stirring across the ocean that would transform their faith lives.

Gumbleton could not claim to have been part of the proceedings. He was occupied with his classes. But like everyone

1. A discussion of the Vatican II condemnation is addressed by Dave Armstrong in "Analysis of *Gaudium et Spes* Regarding Nuclear Strikes," *Patheos*, January 30, 2018.

in Rome he sensed the excitement of history in the making. In Rome he saw firsthand the fervor generated by Pope John XXIII, a pope with a corpulent body and a friendly face, so different from his ascetic, stern-looking predecessors, and by the council he had convened. He had regular opportunities to see the pope, as he addressed public audiences in St. Peter's Square. In the house where he lived he interacted with a stream of visiting theologians and American church officials. Among the luminaries who visited and discussed the events of the day were Father Hans Küng, the German/Swiss who served as one of the theological "experts" who worked with the council fathers. Another expert, Father John Courtney Murray, an American Jesuit, made an enormous contribution to church teaching at the council regarding religious freedom. For a church that had long taught that "error has no rights," and that advocated as an ideal the establishment of an official religion (as long as that was Catholic), Murray's work, so inflected by the experience of the church in the United States, helped usher in a new era. This teaching on the role of conscience was ultimately another area of lasting influence on Gumbleton.[2] By the time he returned to Detroit to pursue his ecclesiastical career, these teachings of Vatican II would have a far greater impact on his outlook than his studies of canon law.

Gumbleton was immediately called to the chancery downtown. Under the leadership of Cardinal John Dearden, the archdiocese was responding vigorously to the changes in the church and the world. Gumbleton was given the title of assistant chancellor and entrusted with great responsibility for archdiocesan operations. Dearden, once known as Iron John for his firm style of administration, came out of Vatican II a transformed leader. While his iron will never wavered, following the council he directed it toward the goal of church renewal. Sometimes he

2. Barry Hudock, "The Fight for Religious Freedom: John Courtney Murray's Role in Dignatitis Humanae," *America*, November 19, 2015.

encountered resistance. But he would have a pivotal impact on the emerging thought of the young priest.[3]

Apart from introducing the liturgical reforms mandated by the council, Dearden also took seriously the call to engagement with the world. In Detroit in the late 1960s that meant addressing race and inequality. The city was spreading outward, with many Catholics leaving the inner city to what became a majority black population. The traditional heart of the archdiocese, the cohort of white ethnic Catholics, was pouring into the suburbs, which were often closed to blacks via overt or covert segregation.

Gumbleton's education on race matters was a gradual process. In his youth, his contact with black people was limited. "In a sense we grew up afraid of black people," he said at a conference on racism in 1996.[4] There was a lone black student at Sacred Heart Seminary, and he had dropped out, most likely, Gumbleton reflected in retrospect, because he had been offered little support and had been expected simply to blend in with his white classmates. As he grew in appreciation of the issue of race, Gumbleton began to analyze what he had done, or not done, in Dearborn. He realized that the parish, by omission, had silently taken the side of those white ethnic Catholics who, having fled Detroit, wanted nothing to do with its black residents. The parish, lively and vibrant in the swirl of school and parish activities, had confronted no social criticism of the situation. That apathy had extended to the young associate pastor.

Nevertheless, he would remember his years in Dearborn fondly. At a time when the church seemed to have an abundance of priests, Gumbleton, as an associate, was blessedly removed from administrative details. Thus, he was able to spend lots of time with parishioners and to enjoy teaching reli-

---

3. Daniel Melody, "Cardinal Dearden Legacy Project Keeps Vatican II Pioneer's Spirit Alive," *Michigan Catholic*, July 26, 2018. Also see Richard McBrien, "Vatican II Themes: The Church as Communion," *National Catholic Reporter*, August 8, 2012.

4. Joseph K. Zyble, "Gumbleton Decries Racism in the Church," *National Catholic Reporter*, November 15, 1996.

gion to the seventh and eighth graders in the parish school. Six decades later, he is still in touch with some of his students. "The school contact is more lasting than others you have in a parish," he said. He grew close to many families. One woman remembers her mother going to the young Father Gumbleton for advice on whether she should be allowed to go to her high school prom. The priest said sure. Sixty years later, the student is still grateful.[5]

Still, amid the rich social and pastoral life of the parish, Gumbleton realizes that he missed much of what was happening beyond the church community. "I look back and am embarrassed and ashamed to admit that at that time I had no social awareness at all," Gumbleton recalled. That was not to last for long.

In 1967, Gumbleton was named pastor at Holy Ghost Parish in northeast Detroit, while also serving in the chancery. At the time, pastorates were rarely offered to the newly ordained. Gumbleton was just thirty-seven, a youthful pastor for the time. But there was a need.

This was the year of the riots in Detroit. Gumbleton, stung by the growing acknowledgment that he had failed to address racism while a busy young priest in Dearborn, felt the church needed to transform its vision of urban ministry. While serving at Holy Ghost, he also worked hard in his chancery job to locate pastors who were willing to tackle civil rights and housing issues, not simply yielding passively in the face of de facto segregation.

"He was not afraid to make moves," recalled Fr. Norman Thomas, Gumbleton's lifelong friend from seminary days. Beginning as Dearden's assistant chancellor, and later rising up to be vice chancellor, Gumbleton moved younger, more progressive pastors into city parishes. Young and brash himself, he was willing to use his position to shake things up.[6]

---

5. Bishop Gumbleton, interview with author, June 2018.
6. Norman Thomas, phone interview with author, 2017.

"He had a lot of authority and he used it to make some good changes," said Norman Thomas, one of the then-young pastors brought in at the time. For a small group of Catholic activists committed to social change in the city, it was an inspiring time.

"At that time there was a lot of hope. The church in Detroit did things to make real the teachings of the council," recalled Immaculate Heart of Mary Sister Suzanne Sattler, another friend of Gumbleton. She said that Dearden trusted his protégé, even allowing him to be quoted in the newspapers, with comments that didn't always place the archdiocese in the best light.[7]

"He (Gumbleton) was used to making bold moves and going in a certain direction and sticking to it," Norman Thomas recalled.[8] That approach wasn't always popular among some of the older clergy. Among other things, Gumbleton implemented policies to restrict the amount of money parishes could put into their schools. The archdiocese was hoping to win state aid, trusting that the legislators and the governor in Lansing would recognize the value of Catholic schools in inner-city Detroit. Meanwhile, Dearden was concerned that schools were eating up parish budgets, particularly as low-paid religious sisters were being replaced by lay faculty who needed at least a subsistence paycheck.

Some schools closed as a result, and there was push back. Even small changes, nothing near what was to happen later, generated arguments that the archdiocese was poised to abandon Catholic school education in poor neighborhoods. It was an argument that Gumbleton himself would invoke when he was on the other side, cut loose from any real direct influence on chancery policies.

In the Detroit of the 1960s, racial justice was the galvanizing issue, and Dearden was eager to take it on. Gumbleton played the role of administrative go-to on thorny questions, joined by his friend, Father Ken Untener, who would later become bishop

---

7. Suzanne Sattler, phone interview with author, 2017.
8. Norman Thomas, phone interview with author, 2017.

of Saginaw, Michigan, and establish himself as one of the most liberal church leaders in the American hierarchy.

Gumbleton embraced the cause of civil rights activism. On one occasion his contribution of $500 to a group with a reputation for militancy earned him an entry in what would become a growing FBI file (as he would discover to his amazement, two decades later). But along with race in the 1960s, there were other causes emerging as well.

Opposition to the widening war in Vietnam was rapidly growing. No longer could Catholics be automatically expected to provide an uncritical source of blind American patriotism. The Berrigan brothers, Fathers Daniel and Philip, and others like them were now out on the front lines of protest. Those protests engulfed Detroit, where a cadre of clergy and lay activists were beginning to work against the war, joining in demonstrations and urging young men to evade or resist the draft. Gumbleton was asked by a superior in the chancery to meet with the increasingly radical priests and tell them to cool it. The protests were creating unease among many conservative Detroit Catholics.

Decades later, Gumbleton remembered the assignment: "'You're about their age, go talk to them and explain it's not good to be out there publicly,'" he recalled. "'We're getting a lot of negative reaction.'" So he went to meetings at Visitation Church in Detroit, intent on finding a way to calm down the nascent movement. But instead he became a convert. Listening to the dissidents' arguments, Gumbleton could see the connection with the message of justice and peace articulated by Pope John and the recent Vatican Council. "By the time the evening was over," Gumbleton recalled, "I was convinced they were right and that I should join the protest. I was changed."[9]

From that point, Gumbleton gradually moved from the role of quiet chancery church official into more politically tinged activism. After being named an auxiliary bishop in 1968, he was

9. Bishop Gumbleton, interview with author, December 2017.

soon making sure that the war was placed on the agenda of the annual meeting of the U.S. bishops. And he had some success. For the first time in American history the Catholic bishops, as a body, issued a statement that was critical (even if only mildly so, as church activists saw it) about a U.S. war effort. Reflexive patriotism was no longer the default Catholic response.

Yet the war continued, and Americans continued to agonize over what to do. CBS news anchor Walter Cronkite returned from a reporting trip in Vietnam and concluded, on air, that America could not win the war. President Lyndon Johnson stunned the nation by announcing that he would not seek a second term in 1968. Hopes rose that the politicians were getting the message. But perhaps the activists overplayed their hand: the assassination of Robert Kennedy, just after winning the Democratic primary in California, followed by riots at the 1968 Democratic convention in Chicago, fed into a public craving for law and order, as well as an end to the war.

Richard Nixon won the 1968 election on a platform of restoring stability to the streets along with a "secret plan" to end the war. Nixon's plan became clearer soon after he was inaugurated in January 1969. He would hand over much of the ground war to the Saigon government while deploying massive American air raids, to be extended throughout North Vietnam and all through Indochina, along with further threats of escalation. As American troops were steadily withdrawn, Nixon was able to maintain a bedrock of public support. But the activist community was unappeased.

The first years of the Nixon administration brought on massive demonstrations. The colleges were wracked. Dinner table conversations, even in Catholic households raised on a solid union of faith and patriotism, were frequently contentious affairs. The divisions grew even more heated following the invasion of Cambodia in May 1970 and the shooting of students by National Guardsmen at Kent State University. For the first time in history, a war came into American homes through nightly television coverage, with images of American casualties as well as the horrors of napalm and bombardment. While many Americans could put Vietnam into the background of their busy lives, the issue hit particularly hard with young men subject to the draft. The colleges and certain professions filled with young men seeking exemptions from conscription. But it was widely expected that Catholic men, reared on the presumption of deference to authority, would be among the pool of those eligible. Conscientious objector status was considered a rare exception, largely granted to groups such as Mennonites, Quakers, and Jehovah's Witness, considered out of the Christian mainstream.

Gumbleton, nevertheless, worked hard to support a conscientious objector ethic among young Catholic men. In public statements, he argued for a more welcoming church stance to those who argued they could not participate in the war. In a piece in the *New York Times* in July 1971, Gumbleton wrote, "Whether we judge this war in the light of the earliest Christian tradition on war, or according to the just war doctrine, I can reach only one conclusion: Our participation in it is gravely immoral."[10]

As he worked with young men opposed to the war, his own attitudes continued to evolve. He found himself increasingly persuaded by arguments that extended beyond the Vietnam War to apply to all war in general. In other words, he was steadily moving toward a pacifist position. Many of the draft boards, run by local communities, consisted of older veterans, many of them Catholic, who had no idea how it was possible for a Catholic to be a conscientious objector. The issue had never seriously been raised before in the United States, outside of a small group of pacifists, mostly associated with the Catholic Worker movement. Dorothy Day, the guiding force of that movement, embraced pacifism and maintained that position throughout World War II, even as some of her male followers

10. Thomas Gumbleton, "On the Morality of the War," *New York Times*, July 2, 1971.

felt the obligation to serve in the fight against the Nazis and Japanese imperialism.[11]

"Most of our draft boards would not accept a Catholic automatically as a C.O. (conscientious objector)," Gumbleton told the *National Catholic Reporter* in an interview published in February 1972.[12] After all, the Catholic Church was not a pacifist church or sect but had traditionally espoused a just-war tradition. Nevertheless, Gumbleton argued that you didn't need to be a total pacifist to be a conscientious objector. Even just-war theory demanded that potential draftees should evaluate whether they could participate in what was increasingly considered a morally dubious war. "The fault is with the law and not the young men who object," Gumbleton wrote in a 1973 column for the *National Catholic Reporter*.[13]

Sometimes the arguments worked; other times they didn't. But the more he publicly talked about conscientious objection, and how Catholic teaching was moving toward an acceptance of pacifism, the more Gumbleton became identified with the antiwar movement. He was acutely aware that antiwar activism was not on the agenda of many of his fellow Catholics. "With our own Catholic people this was still sort of a shocking thing, to get them to realize that it is the duty of a Christian to analyze the policies of the government and perhaps reject them," he said.

Even Gumbleton cautioned that church leaders could not get too far out in front of their own people, particularly since they had long preached a very different message about the Cold War. To suddenly turn against reflexive anticommunism seemed for many to be a stretch, even as the war in Vietnam became more and more unpopular.

---

11. Patricia McNeal, "Catholic Conscientious Objection during World War II," *Catholic Historical Review* 61, no. 2 (April 1975), 222–42.

12. Rick Casey, "Bishops on Bishops on the War," *National Catholic Reporter*, February 11, 1972, 11.

13. Thomas Gumbleton, "Bishop Reports on South Vietnam Visit: Jails Hold Political Prisoners," *National Catholic Reporter*, May 11, 1973.

Gumbleton would speak in Detroit-area Catholic parishes on the topic of nonviolence and would often be greeted by members of Catholics United for the Faith (CUF), a traditionalist group that saw pacifism as contrary to Catholic belief. Gumbleton saw it, by contrast, as an embrace of an early Christian tradition reaffirmed by the universal church at Vatican II.

The U.S. bishops continued to issue carefully worded statements calling upon Catholics to critically question their government when it came to issues of war and peace. As the war raged, the statements gradually became more assertive. In 1971 they called for the end to the war as "a moral imperative of the highest order."[14] Yet their statement left room for both hawks and doves to gather around what was sometimes ambiguous language. Gumbleton became increasingly critical of his fellow bishops, stating that their meetings often bogged down in relatively trivial matters, such as whether Catholics should be allowed to receive Communion in the hand or on the tongue. For many, more traditional Catholics, those were the kinds of questions where bishops offered expertise—in contrast to the quagmire in Southeast Asia. After all, they argued, what bishop had a handle on complex geopolitical and military matters? Better to leave these issues to the generals and the political leadership.

For many antiwar activists, the bishops were late in coming and not forceful enough. Gumbleton, in the *National Catholic Reporter*, argued that the church probably wasn't ready for a strong antiwar response in the late 1960s. The conditioning of Catholics in the mentality of the Cold War was just too strong.

"If we had taken a very strong stand at that point it might have forced a lot of people to stop and think, but I don't think we could have said that all the Catholic people would suddenly turn around and be against this war. There's too much Catholic history preceding it," he said.[15]

---

14. Eleanor Blau, "U.S. Catholic Bishops Call for End to Indochina Bombing," *New York Times*, November 20, 1971.

15. Casey, "Bishops on Bishops on the War."

While many Catholics were reluctant to accept Gumbleton's active antiwar stance, some of his more activist friends felt he didn't go far enough. Among them were the Berrigan brothers. Dan Berrigan, usually noted as the more serene of the duo, castigated Gumbleton for what he considered his inaction. In a letter in the early 1970s, Dan Berrigan told the bishop that he wasn't willing to go far enough in his protest. The issues were too urgent, he said. The bishop should be in jail like other activists, ready to put a spoke in the war machinery. To do anything less was to tolerate a moral abomination, he argued.[16]

Gumbleton was taken aback by the tone of the letter. (At the time he and Berrigan hadn't even met in person.) "It made me somewhat angry and upset. I thought I was being judged unfairly," he told Tom Roberts of the *National Catholic Reporter*.[17]

But Gumbleton didn't toss the letter away. He pondered over it. And, the more he thought, the more he was willing to concede that Berrigan had a point. "I've always felt grateful that he had found the time to write," said Gumbleton, "even though he was being very critical."

Notwithstanding his occasional voice of moderation, as the war dragged on, Gumbleton played the role of gadfly at bishops' meetings, cajoling his fellow bishops to make stronger statements against the ongoing slaughter. A November 1972 *New York Times* article described one such meeting.[18] Nixon had just been reelected in a massive forty-nine-state landslide. There was little appetite among many of the bishops to take on a president who enjoyed solid support from much of their flock. Exit polls indicated that the Catholic vote was a key to Nixon's overwhelming victory. Though Watergate would soon overcome the president's triumph, at the time of the bishops' meeting that still remained on the horizon. Gumbleton wanted

---

16. Tom Roberts, "Soon 75, Berrigan's Is Still an Edgy God," *National Catholic Reporter*, January 26, 1996.

17. Ibid.

18. Eleanor Blau, "Catholic Bishops Ask End of Bombing in Vietnam," *New York Times*, November 17, 1972.

the bishops to issue a statement condemning Nixon's Christmas bombing of Hanoi. The statement the bishops agreed upon, by a 186–4 vote, called upon "a just and lasting peace with security and freedom for all the nations and peoples of Southeast Asia."[19] It was designed as a statement unobjectionable to both hawks and doves alike.

Gumbleton was able to insert a call to condemn both "bombing and terrorism"—the first time he was able to get his fellow bishops to address U.S. policy. (Bombing referred to the regular U.S. air strikes, while the reference to terrorism was a reference to the Vietcong's disruption and killings of civilians in South Vietnam.) The statement quoted John XXIII that in a nuclear age, war was no longer a way to settle disputes.[20]

The floor debate among the bishops echoed what was being said in the rest of the country.

Bishop Robert E. Lucey of Seattle was not optimistic about the call for a negotiated peace. "What good is an agreement with a bunch of Communists that don't want to keep that agreement?" he was quoted in the *New York Times'* coverage of the meeting.[21] Gumbleton, while prodding for more, came away with a sense that the bishops, by acknowledging the bombing, had shown some movement. For his more activist friends, this appeared to be a minor concession.

Even as a young, relatively obscure, auxiliary bishop, Gumbleton was emerging as the hierarchy's most persistent critic of the war. He tried to take on the war by pushing the actual moral constraints imposed by just-war teaching. In the modern age, war was no longer waged as it was in the time of Thomas Aquinas, with soldiers confronting opposing sides on the battlefield. Modern war now inevitably involved mass civilian casualties. This ran up against the just-war criterion of proportionality. Even if an unjust aggressor could be violently opposed,

19. Ibid.
20. Ibid.
21. Ibid.

in doing so, it was necessary that the cost in terms of civilian casualties be weighed against whatever good might result from armed struggle. The argument of antiwar Catholics, especially pacifist critics of Vietnam, was that modern war, with its weapons of mass destruction, offered no hope of meeting the burden of proportionality.

Around this time, Gumbleton was arrested for the first time for an act of civil disobedience. War protestors trespassed at Oscoda Michigan Air Force Base, where pilots were trained for missions in Vietnam. It would be the first of a number of such actions for Gumbleton. Other priests had preceded him. But Gumbleton was the first American bishop to undertake such an action. To many, his action signaled a shake-up in the eternal order. But for Gumbleton, this was a recovery of ancient wisdom. "The Christian tradition going back to the beginning says God's laws must come before human law," Gumbleton recalled decades later.

Nevertheless, he downplayed the significance of his action. "It was like getting a parking ticket," he said, as the ritual of civil disobedience played itself out. He would be put into a jail cell, sent to a hearing, and then released.[22] Still, such actions garnered press attention. Gumbleton, with his status as a bishop, was able to generate attention at a time when such actions had become an old story. Gumbleton's boss, Dearden, never stood in the way. "I never thought of getting permission," said Gumbleton. "If he didn't like it, he would have surely let me know it."

Gumbleton remembered his mentor's words when he was named a bishop. Just be yourself, he had told Gumbleton. Getting arrested in civil disobedience was part of the package. "He was an extraordinary person," Gumbleton recalled about Dearden. One time the archdiocesan newspaper editorialized against a public stance taken by the cardinal. As publisher, Dearden could have demanded the editor's dismissal or a new

22. Bishop Gumbleton, interview with author, December 2018.

editorial. Instead he settled for replying in a letter to the editor, much like any other complaining reader. "You could dialogue with him. I don't think there would be another bishop in the country who would be so open to another point of view," Gumbleton said.

With the signing of the Paris Peace Accords in January 1973, the urgency of Vietnam quickly began to recede for most Americans. Not so for Gumbleton. He was working along with Massachusetts congressman and Jesuit priest Robert Drinan to raise money to rebuild Hanoi's Bach Mai Hospital, recently destroyed during the notorious Christmas bombing raids. Even if American troops were coming home, for the Vietnamese the war and the repression were continuing—still with American backing. With a New England Jesuit, Fr. Robert Manning, then a chaplain at Holy Cross College, he worked on a plan for them both to go to Vietnam and see for themselves what they could do. Manning connected Gumbleton with Don Luce, a Minnesota activist with a particular concern for South Vietnamese political prisoners. These prisoners were held in notorious "Tiger Cages," unable to stand erect for days and weeks at a time. When they were released, they frequently emerged as literally crippled men, unable to walk after their sustained torture.

It wasn't easy to organize such a trip, but eventually their delegation, which also included three Canadians, including Bishop Guy Belanger, was able to visit Vietnam over Easter Week 1973. Gumbleton recalled the visit as an eye opener.

"I really wanted to believe that there were really no political prisoners jailed in Saigon without trial," Gumbleton wrote in the *National Catholic Reporter* upon his return.[23] That was not what he found. He reported that prisoners were subject to inhumane treatment, including torture. The group met with young dissidents, including a group called Young Christian Workers, who included those who had been tortured by the Saigon government for political reasons. He met with Archbishop

23. Gumbleton, "Bishop Reports on South Vietnam Visit."

Paul Nguyen Van Binh of Saigon. Five of the archbishop's own priests had been arrested.

Upon his return Gumbleton described what he had seen and heard to anyone who would listen. He told stories about how, in Vietnam, he had visited with two priests whose churches had been bombed. He visited a family with a son who was born blind and deaf, a casualty of Agent Orange, the defoliant dropped in South Vietnam to clear the jungle to create a favorable fighting terrain for American troops.

Returning to a country tired of the war and now immersed in Watergate political intrigue, Gumbleton's complaints about political prisoners in Saigon failed to make much of an impact. But he continued to remind American Catholics about the impact of the war that never ended for the Vietnamese until the ignominious defeat of the Saigon regime on April 30, 1975, when invading Communists took over Saigon and quickly renamed it Ho Chi Minh City.

For Americans, the war in Vietnam was over, but for Gumbleton the struggle for peace was just beginning. "I would like to see the peace movement as a permanent fixture of American life. The energies and the talents of the millions of people who marched, worked and prayed for peace should not be dissipated in less important pursuits," he wrote in February 1973 for the *National Catholic Reporter*.[24]

Catholic historian David O'Brien, talking to Tom Roberts of the *National Catholic Reporter*, noted that the emergence of Catholic peace activists was an indication of a maturing American Catholic church. "There was a kind of way in which the church in the United States—as a minority church and very anxious to secure a place for itself in the culture—engaged in a patriotism that expressed both its anxiety about its minority status and gratitude for the opportunities, for the successes that the great Catholic middle class achieved," said O'Brien.[25]

24. Ibid.
25. Roberts, "Soon 75."

The activists were willing to point out that perhaps the church had become too comfortable in American culture. While he was talking about Dan Berrigan, O'Brien could very well have been talking about Gumbleton. "(There is) the problem of integrity that arises for the church—it's kind of a Christian perennial—whenever it finds itself at home in any culture," he said. Gumbleton would never give up that critical, prophetic eye.

As the war faded from memory, Americans in general tried to put that painful experience away. The image of helicopters leaving Saigon, the United States facing a military defeat, signaled the beginning of what many critics called a "Vietnam syndrome," a reluctance to exert a superpower's might around the world. The immediate post–Vietnam era was seen as a period of retrenchment, a time when Americans were skittish about entering into world conflicts, becoming more absorbed in domestic issues such as the ongoing Watergate scandal that would eventually topple Richard Nixon.

Gumbleton, as usual, saw the world differently. Other bishops moved on from critiques of American foreign policy. But for the auxiliary bishop from Detroit, it was only the beginning of more to come. His efforts continued to forge a nonviolent witness that could restrain aggressive Cold War policies that he saw threatening, rather than enhancing, peace and democracy around the world.

The heady days of the late 1960s and early 1970s were a time of cementing long-term friendships in the struggle for peace. Leonard Desroches, a Canadian Catholic peace activist, remembers the impact he experienced through an encounter with Gumbleton, who visited the Capuchin Franciscan seminary in Indiana where Desroches was a student in the late 1960s. The memory of that encounter lingered. Years later, when Desroches would be arrested at an antinuclear protest in Canada, he called on Bishop Gumbleton to testify in his trial. Gumbleton gladly appeared for the defense, explaining why some Catholics felt a need to perform civil disobedience in pursuit of disarmament.

By that time, it was an expression of Gumbleton's routine work, making statements in defense of activists around the country and internationally as well.[26]

One couple, Bill and Mary Carry, were parishioners at St. Hugo of the Hills in Bloomfield, one of the wealthiest parishes in the archdiocese, when Gumbleton came to give a talk. "We had been to Catholic schools and universities. We had never heard anyone talk of Catholic nonviolence," recalled Bill, a native New Yorker and former auto executive who described himself at the time as a "garden variety Republican."[27] Their conservative Catholic backgrounds notwithstanding, the couple soon became absorbed in Gumbleton's causes, joining with him in demonstrations and civil disobedience at the White House, nuclear test sites in Nevada, and the School of the Americas in Fort Benning, Georgia, a magnet for protests against U.S. policy in Latin America since the 1980s.

When the couple wondered how their children could experience a Mass with the dynamic social interaction they experienced on those excursions, Gumbleton would come to their home. He would go with the family on camping trips. Mary recalled that the bishop was often the first one up, quietly praying his Office, the daily prayers of a priest.

They recalled Gumbleton as a dynamic preacher, taking to heart the injunction of the Protestant theologian Karl Barth to preach with "a newspaper in one hand, the Gospel in the other," making the connection between today's issues and Christian doctrine.

The couple eventually gravitated to St. Leo's Church in Detroit, where they would participate in liturgies. The music was lively. Unfortunately, as Mary recalls, not only was Gumbleton tone deaf but even his clapping was off the beat.

---

26. Leonard Desroches, phone interview with author, July 2018. See also Michael Valpy, "Trail Detours into Theology as Judge Questions Sanctity of Joan of Arc," *Toronto Globe and Mail*, May 16, 2000.

27. Bill and Mary Carry, phone interview with author, July 2017.

Credit: Courtesy Thomas Gumbleton

This was not his only flaw. "He always had problems with directions. He never knew where he was," recalled Mary. One time, in Washington for a protest, he dropped Bill off at the White House, went to park the car, and was lost for hours in the maze of DC streets.[28]

While the roads remained a maze, Gumbleton regularly continued to inject himself into the wider debates of society. He continued to follow a moral compass, if not a navigational one. The wider society might be clapping to an entirely different beat, but Gumbleton would never forsake his own Christian vision.

28. Ibid.

Chapter 5

The Youngest Bishop

"A doer of the word."

In 1973 the Catholic bishops of the United States debated whether to accept studies on the priesthood compiled by two of its brightest lights, Fathers Andrew Greeley, a sociologist, and Eugene Kennedy, a psychologist.

Their studies examined the emotional lives of American priests. Greeley discovered that they were a largely happy lot, consumed with their work, willing to be of service to the parishes and the wider church they served.[1]

Kennedy emphasized that their studies noted a certain kind of arrested emotional development among priests that carried over into psychological and emotional difficulties in relationships.[2] (He himself later left the priesthood to get married.) Kennedy said that his studies indicated that at least 8 percent of American priests were "maldeveloped," severely neurotic, and even sociopathic. That was the bad news. The good news was that another 8 percent were well-developed men. In the middle were those Kennedy described as undeveloped, not psychologically or emotionally mature.

---

1. "National Opinion Research Center, *The Catholic Priest in the United States: Sociological Investigations,* Andrew M. Greeley and Richard A. Schoenherr, principal investigators (Washington, DC: United States Catholic Conference, 1971).

2. Eugene Kennedy with Victor Heckler, "Catholic Priests in the United States," Psychological Investigations (Washington, DC: U.S. Catholic Conference, 1972).

At the end of the meeting, both priests were called on to summarize their findings. After a few questions from the gathered bishops, they were thanked and dismissed. Nothing was formally done by the bishops about the Kennedy and Greeley studies.

For Gumbleton, these findings signaled a disaster, for which the church would pay an enormous price in the decades to come. Later, he would regularly remind listeners that the roots of the sex abuse crisis could be seen in the lack of response at that 1973 bishops' meeting.

"Nothing was ever done with that report," he later wrote. "If we had changed our seminary formation programs back then, if we had provided developmental programs for priests back then when we were presented with the opportunity, we could have prevented a lot of this, I'm sure. But even now, that's the kind of thing that I hope the bishops . . . will bring about. We do know how to form fully developed people, but it doesn't just happen by magic or by the kind of formation we've had in the seminary."[3]

As the bishops' response indicated, any serious effort to acknowledge or deal with psychological weaknesses among the clergy was considered going too far, even in the heady post–Vatican II days when the church was willing to entertain changes in the area of ministry and liturgy. Especially difficult to face was the admission that priests had sexual issues.

As a young bishop, Gumbleton saw a missed opportunity. As a Detroit chancery official he had seen how heavy a burden celibacy posed for many clergy. He noted the issues with alcoholism. He was often the last stop on the way out as priests confided in him why they made the decision to leave the priesthood, a common occurrence in the late 1960s and into the 1970s.

The secrecy in which bishops operated often ran against the

---

3. Bishop Gumbleton on priesthood formation, interview with author, December 2017.

insights of modern psychology. Gumbleton had seen it in his own rise.

One day in 1968 Gumbleton received a letter from the apostolic nuncio that he was going to be named a bishop. Only thirty-eight, Gumbleton felt he was too young and inexperienced to accept such a heavy responsibility. Other priests might have been delighted to move up through the ranks, but Gumbleton seemed to regard himself as an accidental bishop. He was about to be named the youngest man in the U.S. Catholic hierarchy. It made him uncomfortable. What is more, the call came at a difficult time.

"Why am I staying around?," Gumbleton had been asking himself about his own vocation to the priesthood. Many of his contemporaries had abandoned the clerical state. As he approached middle age, he found himself having his own doubts.[4] Many of his priest friends were now married and out of active ministry. Gumbleton carefully weighed his options and thought maybe he would one day join them. Being called to be a bishop would seem to close off that option. The call confronted him with the burden of a heavy choice. Once he accepted, there would be no easy way to opt out, like other ex-priests. Should he stay or should he go? It had come down to grappling with celibacy.

All through those years of seminary training, from the time as a fourteen-year-old when he entered Sacred Heart, Gumbleton clearly understood that to become a priest would mean giving up the possibility of marriage. It was part of the deal. But having any great insight into the celibate life and what that entailed only developed as he went along. For outsiders, celibacy was the strange jewel in the crown of the Catholic clergy. It was intriguing, in its own way. Who would willingly give up the comforts of hearth, home, and a sexual relationship for a particular ministry in the church? Greeley, for one, regularly confronted this issue in his sociological writings and novels.

4. Bishop Gumbleton, interview with author, December 2017.

For its defenders, celibacy was a sign of the kingdom, a witness lived out in a daily struggle, showing that the demands of the gospel were worth sacrificing for.

Yet the reality was often far from a romantic ideal. From personal experience, Gumbleton knew that priests often were burdened and ill-prepared to deal with celibacy or the demands of pastoral leadership. Many resorted to alcohol to cope with their loneliness. As a chancery official called in to mediate difficult disputes between parishioners and pastors, Gumbleton knew from hard experience that the emotional health of priests was often the issue.

"That's what was happening. You could have corrected a lot of problems back then," he would later recall, in light of the sex abuse crisis that would wrack the church in subsequent decades. But this was a time when clergy were still considered far above the human fray, and psychological intervention was often considered out of bounds for men who were consecrated in a special way in service to God and the church. "Look where we are now? Back then we could have saved some," Gumbleton said, reflecting on the dwindling number of young men attracted to the priesthood. In 2017 the archdiocese celebrated only three ordinations (Gumbleton's class had more than thirty), not nearly enough to replace those priests retiring or leaving active ministry.[5]

Meanwhile, those who were now attracted to the priesthood often espoused the ideal of separateness and specialness among the clergy, a resurgence of attitudes that Gumbleton had grown up with in pre–Vatican II days. Younger priests were again embracing the attitude that they were "ontologically" changed by their ordination. Once more they liked to dress in cassocks and distinctive clerical garb, a sign of being set apart from their ordinary flock.

Pope Francis, otherwise famous for being nonjudgmental, has been quick to decry expressions of clericalism. He even

5. *Michigan Catholic*, October 5, 2017.

described young clerics who lorded it over lay people as "little monsters." But few dioceses in the United States seemed to be listening to such concerns. The old seminary system continued pretty much as it always did, albeit with many fewer potential priests coming through the pipeline.

Those issues were not new. They weighed on Gumbleton when he was called to be a bishop in 1968. It was a turning point, a time when he was forced to consider the role of celibacy in his life in a serious way, for the first time. Besides, he felt he was just too young. There were other more deserving clergy, those with far more pastoral experience, who were better prepared to do this work. Gumbleton at the time had just barely spent time as a pastor, having moved from an associate's job in Dearborn to the life of a chancery official. He knew that there would be resentment from his clerical peers who were older and, he thought, more ready to take on the role of bishop.

"I knew I had to make a choice. If I said yes I would not leave the priesthood. At that point I knew what I was accepting," recalled Gumbleton decades later about that time of personal turmoil.[6]

The rules around such appointments were strict. The process of selecting bishops needed to be confidential. Having received the phone call, Gumbleton was allowed a few days to consider, but he knew that the rules required him to keep the future appointment secret. He was not allowed to talk about it with friends or family.

Gumbleton figured he would use Dearden as his confessor; that was one exception allowed under the rules of confidentiality. Even so, the cardinal was not known to be warm and fuzzy. Gumbleton knew that his boss had a regular routine, beginning with public mornings at meetings, but his afternoons were spent in his office, secluded from the rest of the staff. It was his time to recollect, and his staff knew not to disturb him. That afternoon, Gumbleton violated the custom and knocked on the door.

---

6. "The Bishop as Victim, *Toledo Blade,* January 19, 2006, A10.

Dearden said he had no idea that his young protégé had been selected to be a bishop. Nevertheless, it couldn't have come as a complete surprise; he had to have at least put in a positive word about Gumbleton, which had evidently resonated with those in the complex Vatican bureaucracy that oversaw the selection of bishops.

Dearden offered the young cleric advice: be yourself, say yes, and do it. Dearden emphasized that bishops were human, too, and that they experienced struggles as much as the average layman in a challenging marriage or a pastor having second thoughts about celibacy. But there was a new kind of church emerging that could use Gumbleton's gifts. His administrative skills had been recognized by the appointment. It was now up to the young priest to accept it. He was duty bound and was as qualified as anyone else could have been, Dearden told him.

Reluctantly, Gumbleton agreed. On March 4, 1968, in Detroit's Blessed Sacrament Cathedral, fewer than a dozen years since his ordination as a priest, Gumbleton was consecrated a bishop. Newspaper reports about the event focused on his youth.

In a homily more than a half century later, Gumbleton reflected on that time. He remembered spending time on some of the ceremonials of being a new bishop, including the selection of his motto. He knew he had to pick out a motto, a summary of how he understood his episcopal ministry. He went to the Kenedy Directory, a listing of all church institutions and dioceses around the country. He started with Alaska. The first bishop he ran across had chosen "Be doers of the word, not hearers."

"I thought, that's not bad; that could be because I already had been involved in public activities and social justice and so on. So I thought yes, I'll take that motto," he remembered. "But I never realized how challenging it really would be to try to live up to that, to be a doer of the word." "Being a doer of the word means taking all of the Scriptures, everything in these Scriptures, very seriously. You make them part of your life—doers of the word, not hearers. It also means not only the scriptures, but Jesus," he said.

At age thirty-eight he was the youngest bishop in the United States. He was clearly on the ascent and would move up the hierarchical ladder. Under the wing of Dearden, then a powerful church figure, the young bishop would surely land his own diocese in the near future. That's the way things generally worked in the way of episcopal careers. At the time, Gumbleton had no indication that, career-wise, he would stagnate in essentially the same church rank he had attained before achieving middle age. He would remain an auxiliary bishop, never leaving his hometown, with an office within miles of his childhood home on Manor Street.

Gumbleton would live and die as a bishop, but with the title of auxiliary beside it, an indication that he would never be his own boss, always tied directly to the authority of the archbishop of Detroit. Early on, Dearden told him that he could expect to move on to lead his own diocese. Dearden's successor, Cardinal Edmund Szoka, who took over the archdiocese in 1981 upon Dearden's retirement, told him the same thing.

Szoka, appointed by John Paul II, offered an ideologically different take on Dearden's progressive confidence. Dearden would sponsor giant conferences, such as Call to Action, where various strands of the church, including those who desired women's ordination and openness to sexual minorities, could have their forum, even if Dearden himself was unwilling to go that far. Szoka, a bespectacled, quiet man with the demeanor of an astute bookkeeper, forged a reputation for his ability to handle money.[7] It was a gift he later parlayed into a position at the Vatican in charge of the church's finances. Szoka was quick to tell Gumbleton that he could expect to have his own diocese at some future date. There might have been some self-interest involved. Gumbleton knew that he had become an ecclesial

---

7. Thomas Reese, "Cardinal Edmund Szoka, a Remembrance," *National Catholic Reporter*, August 25, 2014.

thorn in the side. Szoka may well have been expressing a hope, not so much a reality, that he would eventually be free of a troublesome auxiliary.

But as appointments to other dioceses were regularly filled, Gumbleton was conspicuously left behind. An unusually soft-spoken man, averse to crudity, Gumbleton recognized that he had landed on what might politely be called a negative Vatican list, either formally or, just as probable, informally. He knew, as the church moved into the era of Pope John Paul II, that his brand of social justice activism was not appreciated any more in the higher echelons of the American hierarchy than it was at the Vatican.

At first, he bristled at the realization. Others were being raised up, at least some with apparently lesser intellectual gifts. But eventually he let go of such thoughts. Gradually, a sense of liberation took over, freeing him to look at his episcopal vocation in an entirely different light. He wouldn't be trapped by the ever-present pressure to conform. He knew he wasn't going anywhere. He loved Detroit, and so remaining in his hometown was not a hardship. In foregoing any ambition of moving up the ecclesial ladder, he was free to pursue social justice causes that other bishops in charge of dioceses either did not have the time for or were reluctant to embrace, fearful of alienating key church supporters. His official role in the archdiocese was to help organize the ministry in urban parishes, a job he relished, and one that allowed for flexibility in pursuing a wider national and international agenda.

He developed alliances with a dwindling number of fellow bishops who shared his ideological disposition toward social justice and an evolving pacifism. One of these comrades in the hierarchy, Bishop Walter Sullivan of Richmond, Virginia, was as stalwart in causes such as nuclear disarmament as he was. But as leader of a diocese, Gumbleton knew that his friend was more tied down. Sullivan had large military bases in his diocese, Catholics to whom he ministered, and who would not be appreciative of a pacifist bishop. Sullivan made many statements about the issues, but his involvement in organizations and in actions such as civil disobedience were necessarily more circumscribed than those of the auxiliary bishop from Detroit.

"As an auxiliary I had more freedom," Gumbleton recalled. Dearden, for one, never objected to his activism. Even Szoka, known for his financial acumen and conservative bent, never tried to bring Gumbleton to task for his participation in social justice causes from disarmament to opposition to American policy in Central America during the Reagan years.

After years of tackling the issues bedeviling the wider society, Gumbleton became more outspoken about internal church issues. In 1989 he even joined in a protest in front of the cardinal's house, in a protest against Szoka's wholesale closing of parishes in Detroit and some of its suburbs. It was a time of intense tension in the archdiocese, as Gumbleton and a small band of priests, largely centered in urban Detroit, reacted strongly to the effort to close down much of the church's presence in the city.[8]

Szoka, at least in his dealings with a fellow bishop, was a no-hard-feelings kind of person. He would make a point at a meeting but would then be sure to be friendly and gregarious afterward. Gumbleton appreciated that. But he still went on with his regular protests and activism.

The closings were a sore point. Forty-two parishes were closed in the first wave. Most were from the inner city. It was seen by critics as a massive sellout by the archdiocese, away from its former city base in favor of the suburbs. Well before the church would have to deal with giant sex abuse settlements, Szoka was moving the church into retrenchment, a pattern that would repeat itself throughout the industrial Midwest and the Northeast in decades to come. The church was losing its grip where it had once been strong. Szoka was seen by his supporters as being able to recognize reality and make adjustments. For his detractors, he was moving the church to a more comfortable base.

8. David Crumb, "Discussions on Church Closings Quickly Turn into Protests," *National Catholic Reporter*, March 17, 1989.

Detroit turned out to be a trendsetter. Perhaps that was because the issues in Detroit were so stark. Catholics had joined the massive move to the suburbs in most American cities. The urban neighborhood parish, where people walked to Mass, was dying. Nowhere was this more evident than in Detroit. The old city parishes continually relied on suburban pilgrims with links to the old neighborhoods. That population was declining and graying. While black Catholics constituted a substantial minority in the archdiocese, most black immigrants from the American South had their roots in the Protestant churches. By the late 1980s the city was increasingly dotted with evangelical and independent churches, some in storefronts and others in larger buildings. The Catholic presence was seen as withering away.

Still Gumbleton, who had run into his own issues with closures when he worked for Dearden, was outraged. From his perspective at St. Leo's, there was no need to close most Detroit parishes. His parish was spared, largely due to Gumbleton's status as a bishop. This was where he carried out his ministry, and he was adamant that it was worthwhile to continue, even if the numbers and the collections were not what they were.

Catholic bishops are part of a tight-knit club. Gumbleton, by joining the protests against Szoka's parish closings, was publicly violating the rules of the club. Not only did he participate in protests, an act unheard of by a bishop against his own archdiocese, but he also testified in favor of a city council resolution to investigate the impact of the church closings on the city, particularly in the realm of social services. The archdiocese saw the city council discussions as meddling and an infringement on its religious liberty.[9] Gumbleton argued that the city council's interest was a warm testament to the church's social impact among the poor of the city. It was an act of appreciation. In any case, it was ineffective. The closures continued.

---

9. Ibid.

By 2018, the city of Detroit contained forty-two parishes, compared to 129 when Gumbleton was ordained. There were only four Catholic elementary schools, compared to 109 in 1956. Catholic high schools dropped from fifty-four to three. Some parishes remained as centers of vibrant ministry, combining the black Catholic tradition of the Gospel Mass, like St. Charles Borromeo and Sacred Heart, where Gumbleton's old friend Norman Thomas was pastor for decades.

Still, Gumbleton saw the closures as a failure of imagination. "You don't have to have large numbers to keep a parish going," he said, noting that St. Leo's proved that. Parishioners were known and welcomed. If they missed Mass for a few weeks, they got a phone call, wondering if there was anything wrong. If the food stamps ran out, there were food pantries. There were few institutions in the city that could provide that kind of grassroots care.

Some critics saw Szoka's motives as financial, allowing the archdiocese, like a giant corporation, to lop off branch offices that were becoming a money drain. But there was another issue: the precipitous decline in the number of clergy. According to the Archdiocese of Detroit archives, by 2018, there were 343 archdiocesan priests, compared to more than a thousand when Gumbleton was ordained.

"It was the priest problem. We weren't going to have enough," said Gumbleton. Better to consolidate resources in the suburbs, where most of the Catholics had gone. The city itself had been losing its population for decades. The population of Detroit in 2018 was 677,000, a drastic decline from the 1.8 million residents who had occupied the city when Gumbleton was growing up. And in this new century, fewer Detroit residents were Catholics; fewer still were in the pews on Sunday mornings.

Like a good financial manager, Szoka was willing to pare down troubled assets. All Gumbleton and his friends in urban parishes could do was to raise their voices in collective protest. But the parish closings continued.

Chapter 6

No More Vietnam Syndrome

"He never learned to speak bishopese."

For about a month in early 1980, Gumbleton found it difficult to go into a restaurant without someone offering to pay for his meal. At a time of intense tension, the auxiliary bishop of Detroit earned a celebrity status, even if he was still a *persona non grata* for many in the U.S. government. It was all part of what may have been the most intense period of public scrutiny he ever experienced.

Once the Vietnam War was over, the contentious issues that had divided American Catholics tended to fade into the backdrop. But not for Gumbleton. Throughout his career, his activism sharpened and his public comments became even more controversial. He seldom refused a press interview, seeing journalists as a potential forum for delivering his views. He spoke regularly to reporters from the Detroit dailies, the *Free Press* and the *News*, as well as the gamut of the Catholic press, from the friendly *National Catholic Reporter* to the *Wanderer*, an ultraconservative publication that regularly wrote negative pieces about the auxiliary bishop. This openness to the press was a rarity among bishops, who often viewed the Fourth Estate as instigators of discord, best ignored unless absolutely necessary. His church superiors noticed. Nevertheless, Gumbleton's tendency to engage the press had begun early in his career.

After an interview with *The Critic* magazine in the late 1960s, during which Gumbleton voiced candid opinions on social and church issues, he received a friendly warning letter from Archbishop Jean Jadot, the apostolic delegate to the United States, suggesting that bishops stay away from press interviews. Jadot became famous for helping to reshape the American church hierarchy in the post–Vatican II era. He brought in younger, more progressive figures. He undoubtedly had influence on the appointment of Gumbleton as a bishop, who in this case chose to ignore his counsel.

"I was shocked that Jadot would say you should back off. I didn't take his advice," said Gumbleton.[1]

By contrast, Dearden, his mentor, was willing to grant Gumbleton space. This was true even when Gumbleton spoke out on local issues, always the most contentious for bishops who had to face complaints in their trips around the diocese. The issue of race around Detroit was particularly sensitive. Gumbleton suggested to one of the Detroit dailies that the archdiocese, much like the public schools of the region, use busing to integrate its schools. The story landed on the front page of the *Free Press*'s Sunday edition, the most prominent local news-space in the pre-internet era. Dearden took some flak with angry phone calls the following morning.

"He never learned to speak bishopese," said Father Norman Thomas, pastor of Sacred Heart Church in Detroit, and a longtime friend of Gumbleton, dating to seminary days.[2]

Described as the pastor of the Catholic peace and justice movement, Gumbleton lived in Detroit nearly his entire life, yet his influence was felt in far-flung places such as El Salvador, Haiti, Vietnam, Iran, and Iraq, wherever he felt called to provide a gospel witness against violence and repression. Often there would be a reporter accompanying him, in particular hot spots, such as Iran, sometimes more than one. He was step-

1. Bishop Gumbleton, interview with author, June 2018.
2. Norman Thomas, phone interview with author, 2017.

ping far out of the public relations boundaries for an auxiliary bishop. It was an increasingly uncomfortable place, both inside and outside the church.

Shaken by what many commentators described as Vietnam syndrome, American policy in the 1970s began to retrench. There was a reluctance to exercise Cold War strategies through aggressive interventions around the world. On top of the Vietnam War, the Watergate scandal and subsequent congressional investigations into the CIA had left their scars. The revelation that the CIA had engineered coups and even planned the assassination of foreign leaders repulsed many Americans.

The election of Jimmy Carter in 1976 promised a foreign policy built on respect for human rights. The United States began to be perceived as more of a grand international mediator, as reflected in the success Carter achieved in bringing together Anwar Sadat and Menachem Begin to sign an Egyptian–Israeli peace treaty in 1978. The deal between two former antagonists, witnessed by the smiling Carter, offered a promise that perhaps even the Middle East could find a pathway to harmony. The promise of good feeling was not to last long.

When Soviet troops invaded Afghanistan in late 1979, Carter responded by increasing the U.S. military budget and canceling American involvement in the Moscow Olympics of 1980. The Cold War was coming back with a vengeance, with Carter routinely portrayed as naïve and out of his depth in confronting the evils of the Soviet empire.

If there was ever a chance that a gentler approach to foreign policy might have a chance, that hope seemed to crash on November 4, 1979, when an Iranian mob, seemingly with the support of the new revolutionary Islamic government, took over the American embassy in Teheran, eventually holding fifty-two Americans hostage for 444 days.

The reaction in the United States was intense. Walter Cronkite of CBS News ended each one of his high-rated broadcasts by rattling off the number of days the hostages had been held. (This was during a time when the three major broadcast networks were the major source of international news for most Americans.) ABC News developed a highly rated nighttime newscast that competed with Johnny Carson, largely focused on events in Iran. During the 444 days of the crisis, the hostages and their families became national celebrities.[3] The small towns and big cities where they had their roots were draped in yellow ribbon (a reference to a pop song of the day about welcoming home a prisoner). The Iranians portrayed the hostages as duplicitous tools of CIA intrusion into their lives, playing off the recent memory of the U.S. role in installing and propping up the hated Shah of Iran.

But the American public was having none of that viewpoint. Combined with the travails of a difficult economy, the hostage crisis resulted in an end to Carter's hopes of reelection and the ascension of Ronald Reagan, who promised to implement a tougher U.S. foreign policy. A fervent brand of nationalism was once again taking hold in the United States. There were few voices in opposition. Into all this national agitation strode the auxiliary bishop of Detroit.

That Christmas, American television news captured the image of a lone Catholic bishop getting on a plane to visit the hostages in Iran. He was bringing words of consolation to the Americans held captive while at the same time offering an olive branch to their captors. Gumbleton was once again on the move, ready to insert himself into an international controversy. It was an accidental intervention.

Archbishop John Quinn of San Francisco, then president of the U.S. bishops' conference, had asked the State Department if they would authorize religious services for the hostages in Iran for Christmas. The answer was a resounding no.[4]

At the time, Gumbleton was living at St. Teresa's rectory in Detroit. The phone rang. It was Daniel Berrigan, the Jesuit priest

---

3. Dylan Rosenfeld, "The Portrayal of the Iran Hostage Crisis by American Media," *Vanderbilt Historical Review*, November 8, 2016.

4. Bishop Gumbleton, interview with author, December 2018.

and antiwar activist. He had been asked by a University of Kansas professor with connections to Iranian students if he would be willing to go to Iran to visit the hostages. Berrigan had scheduling issues, but wanted to know if Gumbleton would take his place. (Their relationship had warmed in the years since Berrigan had written a scathing letter to the bishop, accusing him of not doing enough for the cause of peace in Vietnam.) The bishop answered yes and was soon on a series of flights that eventually landed in Teheran, with a delegation that included William Sloane Coffin, the activist pastor of Riverside Church in New York City. In his possession was a note from the family of Joe Subic, a young soldier from the Detroit area, who was one of the hostages. Their plane landed around 11:30 p.m. in Teheran, and they were immediately sent to a meeting with the student hostage takers.

The expectation was that they would perform one ecumenical service for the Americans. But the student leaders, apparently worried about security, wanted the pastors to meet with smaller groups. As the negotiations continued, with Coffin taking the lead for the American delegation, the atmosphere grew tense. Gumbleton looked around the room. He noticed a group of nervous young men with guns. He worried that they might be prone to panic. They didn't look particularly well trained. Gumbleton was led into a small room where he was met by a handful of hostages. One, by sheer luck, was Subic. Gumbleton offered greetings from his family in Detroit. Subic was just nineteen, and he looked frightened. There was another soldier, this one from Wisconsin, who was also just nineteen. Another older man came in. He was Jewish. Gumbleton asked in an apologetic tone if he would mind if he led a Christmas service. "I don't care what you do. I am just glad to get out of there," the Jewish hostage told the bishop. Gumbleton led them in prayers and Eucharist, and was greeted by other small groups, including Lutherans and Anglicans, both embassy personnel and others who were simply in the embassy at the wrong time when the students invaded.

The simple prayer services were a highlight in the biggest story of the day. The religious leaders were among only a handful of Westerners who had any contact with the hostages during their captivity. Four days later, the delegation returned to the United States, landing in Washington, DC. The State Department had vociferously objected to their journey, fearing it would feed into propaganda by the Iranian government. But upon their return, the group was welcome to tell what they knew. They reported that the hostages appeared to be in decent physical shape but were obviously scarred by the experience.

The State Department's anxiety about the trip did not extend to the general public. The trip was intensely chronicled by the media. "It seemed like everyone in the country knew about it," Gumbleton recalled. For that week after his return, total strangers would pick up the check at restaurants. A gas station attendant in Detroit declined to charge him for his gas. The hunger on the part of Americans to make any connection with the hostages was met by the bishop and his group, even if the government's reaction was icy.

Gumbleton was not used to being the object of so much appreciation. Nevertheless, he would not let this inhibit him from critiquing U.S. foreign policy. Aside from his meeting with the hostages in Tehran, he had also spoken with the students holding the embassy. He heard their complaints about the U.S. government's role in 1954 in overthrowing an elected regime to impose the Shah on Iran, a policy designed to secure a vital oil link to the world. Many of the students, he said, were reacting to the cruelties imposed by the Shah's regime, including the imprisonment of political prisoners and torture.

During that visit, at the height of U.S.–Iran tensions, he apologized for U.S. support of the deposed Shah, noting that "part of our Catholic tradition is confession of our sins and reparation." At a time of intense patriotic emotion, that part of Gumbleton's visit did not go over well in many quarters.

Gumbleton's respect for religious tradition made him more sympathetic to the Iranians. The Shah, he noted, was a secularizing influence on a country with deep religious roots. He later told the *National Catholic Reporter*: "There is a religious reaction, perhaps more difficult for people to understand because we accept the complete separation of church and state."[5]

The Iranian reaction to the Shah's Western ways was akin to the reaction he saw back in Detroit among some traditionalist Catholics opposed to the changes after Vatican II. He observed much of the same kind of intense emotion regarding what outsiders would perceive as insignificant religious customs.

"When the Shah set out to westernize the country, that meant to religious Iranians a modernizing, an actual crushing out of religious and spiritual things they held very sacred." He continued: "When people can't understand the Iranians' feelings, I remind them of the turmoil that can occur in the Catholic church about apparently minor changes in religious practice."

Those were controversial statements. But they largely got lost in the general admiration for the delegation's efforts. Meanwhile the crisis ended with the release of the hostages—timed by the Iranian government, as a final snub to the outgoing Carter administration—on January 20, 1981, the day of Ronald Reagan's inauguration. The incoming Reagan administration claimed an early PR victory, which cleared the way for action on another series of international fronts. Among them was Central America.

At the time of the Iran crisis, there was another issue brewing much closer to home in the impoverished nations of Central America, particularly Nicaragua and El Salvador. First, Nicaragua, where a long-running, American-supported dictator, Anastasio Somoza, was overthrown by a group of revolutionaries who called themselves Sandinistas, in honor of Augusto Sandino, an early twentieth-century patriot who at one time fought American Marines occupying the country. The war was intense and bloody. By the time the Sandinistas declared

5. Patty Edmonds, "Professor, Bishop Fear U.S. Isn't Listening to Iranians," *National Catholic Reporter*, February 28, 1980.

victory in 1979, many in the United States were seeing a repetition of the Cuban Revolution in 1959—another nationalistic insurrection that had become a pawn on a Cold War chessboard. But now there was a new angle: many Catholics were supporting the revolutionary cause.

The roots of this development lay in a steady process of conversion of the Catholic Church in Latin America, prompted by reflection on the spirit of Vatican II in light of the overwhelming conditions of inequality and oppression in the continent. At a meeting of the Latin American bishops in Medellín, Colombia, in 1968, and then in Puebla, Mexico, in 1979, the church had articulated what became known as a "preferential option for the poor"—a dramatic break from a tradition going back to the original Spanish colonizers that had drawn a close alliance between the church and the ruling elite. That alliance had been strengthened in the struggle against communism. But in the light of brutal military dictatorships that swept the continent in the 1960s and 1970s, as well as the evident conditions of injustice, the church had undergone a change. Articulating the meaning of this change was a theological movement called "liberation theology." Reading the gospel from the perspective of the poor and oppressed, priests, religious, and lay people began to support the call for radical, and even revolutionary change. Biblical themes such as the Exodus story, in which God heard the cry of the oppressed Hebrew slaves and engineered their liberation, took on a new meaning. They reexamined texts from the gospels that had long been seen in pietistic, other-worldly terms, such as Mary's hymn in Luke's Gospel, known as the "Magnificat." Mary praises God (Luke 1:46-55):

> He has put down the mighty from their thrones,
> And has exalted the lowly.
> He has filled the hungry with good things,
> And the rich he has sent away empty. (1:52–53)

This message burned through Central America, a region still stuck in a feudal system, with rich landowners, supported by

American business interests, profiting off the labor of low-paid peasants.

The currents running through Central America, particularly with the successful insurrection in Nicaragua, challenged Gumbleton's pacifism. Around that time he gave a talk in Cleveland, urging a nonviolent course, even against unjust oppression. He was confronted by a nun, just returned from El Salvador, who wondered how Salvadorans could respond in a peaceful manner to the atrocities they were being subjected to, the massive murders and destruction of entire villages carried out by governments under the banner of fighting Marxism.[6] Later on, Gumbleton remembered the nun's name. It was Ursuline Sister Dorothy Kazel, one of the four churchwomen from the United States who would later be murdered by military forces in El Salvador. In the Cold War battlefield of the time, Honduras largely held its ground and became a center of American military intervention during the era. But Nicaragua had already fallen to the Sandinistas, who were seen moving closer and closer to the Soviet bloc, much as Fidel Castro had done in Cuba. The focus of the world was on El Salvador, the only nation named for Jesus himself, as the next focus of upheaval. A guerrilla army was in the field, fighting a Salvadoran military infamous for its brutality and human rights abuses.

Catholic leaders who took sides with the poor soon became targets of government-sponsored death squads. First came Fr. Rutilio Grande, a Jesuit pastor and a charismatic leader, who was murdered in 1977; other priests followed; and then the Archbishop of San Salvador, Oscar Romero, was slain while celebrating Mass at a simple hospital chapel; and then four American church women, three nuns and a young lay missioner, were brutally killed in December 1980.

When the Reagan administration ascended to power, a top priority was to prop up the government of El Salvador in the midst of an expanding civil war, and to try to roll back the

---

6. Ibid.

Credit: Rick Reinhard

Sandinista government in Nicaragua by organizing and supplying anti-Sandinista rebels, called "Contras." The Contras, based in Honduras and Costa Rica, engaged in wide-scale attacks on civilians who support the revolutionary government, including teachers and medical workers.

The cause of Central America remained close to Gumbleton, who over the years made numerous trips with activist groups monitoring the situation in both El Salvador and Nicaragua until peace finally came to the region with peace accords in the early 1990s.

Before that time, in 1987, as hope for peace was beginning to emerge for Salvadoran refugees who had been forced into Honduras by the fighting in their country, one group of peasants, living in a refugee camp in Honduras, sought to return. But traveling through El Salvador, with the threat of being perceived as rebel sympathizers, was a dangerous proposition.

Up stepped Gumbleton. Upon the request of Eileen Purcell, a church worker in San Francisco, California, whose husband was Salvadoran, he agreed to join a caravan heading back to El Salvador, hoping that the presence of American observers would offer some measure of protection. Their village, Corral de Piedra, now known as Comunidad Ellacuría, had suffered greatly from the war. An army helicopter had dropped a bomb through the only stone building in the village. It was a community meeting place used to grind corn. Fourteen died in the explosion. The villagers wanted to return home. At the same time, they were terrified.

The group was led by a Salvadoran named José Artiga. As the caravan approached the border of a province considered a no-go zone by the military, they were confronted by a Salvadoran army unit. Gumbleton, dressed in civilian garb, chatted up some American soldiers who were among the Salvadoran soldiers. They admitted to the bishop that they really were not supposed to be there, but they definitely were.

As the stalemate continued, Artiga organized a songfest and speeches. Gumbleton looked at the Salvadoran soldiers, many of them nervous young men with guns. The thinking was that the soldiers would never kill an American in that situation. But no one could totally bank on that. They had killed Americans in the past. It was an isolated jungle area. Young and nervous men with weapons did not engender a sense of security.

Sister Suzanne Sattler, Gumbleton's friend, remembers the bishop gathering the villagers together in prayer. She said it had an impact on the entire scene. After hours of stalemate, the soldiers lowered their guns. The caravan moved on. The villagers returned home—a quiet victory in a civil war that killed tens of thousands.[7]

---

7. Suzanne Sattler, phone interview with author, 2017.

Chapter 7

The Challenge of Peace

"It's clear moral theology. Once you have the intention to do it you have already committed a sin."

At the national bishops' meeting in November 1980, Bishop P. Francis Murphy, auxiliary of Baltimore, offered a proposal that the bishops take a look at American nuclear weapons policy in the light of the increased tensions of the Cold War, the arms build-up of the later Carter years, and the promises of the incoming Reagan administration to up the ante on the arms race.

Attention soon focused on the U.S. bishops' most ardent pacifist, Bishop Thomas Gumbleton, who was invited to take a leading role. Gumbleton opposed the use and possession of all nuclear weapons, but in the end he was willing to sign on to a document that allowed for maintaining a nuclear deterrence as long as the nation was moving in the direction of disarmament.

"I can never say because I am a pacifist, everybody else must be a pacifist," he said.[1] Personal conscience was his creed. Gumbleton was willing to grant others a wide array of viewpoints, as long as they followed an informed conscience. Gumbleton's work on the committee that drafted this pastoral letter remains one of his lasting contributions to Catholic social teaching.

1. Interview with Bishop Thomas Gumbleton, June 2018.

The context behind the bishops' deliberation was a time of intense agitation around the issue of nuclear weapons. The incoming Reagan administration was clearly signaling its intention to ratchet up opposition to the Soviet Union, with plans to invest in new weapons systems and to deploy nuclear weapons in Europe. The rhetoric and saber rattling of the new administration, and the rise of renewed Cold War tensions, prompted widespread fear and protest. The defense strategy of the day was the threat of "mutually assured destruction," the willingness and preparation of the United States to deter any Soviet attack by threatening a massive retaliation that would leave both sides devastated. This deterrent threat was supposed to keep the world safe. But it meant that U.S. missiles had to be kept on a hair-trigger alert, always vulnerable to false alarms or mistakes. Once the missiles were launched, there was no calling them back.

A million protesters marched in New York City to promote what they called a "Nuclear Freeze," a ban on further production of new weapons along with negotiations to reduce their number. ABC television produced a highly rated movie, *The Day After*, which imagined how a slice of Kansas might experience the consequences of a nuclear Armageddon. Dr. Helen Caldicott, an Australian physician, traveled the world presenting well-attended talks warning of imminent nuclear catastrophe.

Into this maelstrom came the U.S. bishops, at the time quite willing to explore a Catholic response to various international moral issues. At the top of the list had to be nuclear weapons. There was no other greater source of potential worldwide catastrophe. As the arguments became more heated, Catholics wondered whether they could provide an alternative to all the bellicose and dangerous talk emanating out of Washington and Moscow. Could Catholic social teaching offer a way out for a world that many believed was lurching toward catastrophe?

A committee was selected by the bishops' conference, then headed by Archbishop John Roach of Minneapolis–St. Paul, to come up with a statement on the morality of the possession and potential use of nuclear weapons. The committee would have five bishop members, including the chair, Archbishop Joseph Bernardin of Chicago. Two years younger than Gumbleton, he had also, with his consecration as an auxiliary bishop in 1966, become for a time the youngest bishop in America. Unlike, Gumbleton, he had made a quick ascent up the church ladder, serving as the first general secretary of the National Conference of Catholic Bishops from 1968 to 1972. He later became archbishop of Cincinnati before becoming archbishop of Chicago. Considered the consummate church politician, Bernardin was known for his skill in crafting documents that played to the middle, forging consensus among disparate perspectives. He was expected to play that same role with this committee.

Two members of the committee were lesser-known bishops, George A. Fulcher of Lafayette, Indiana, and Daniel P. Reilly of Norwich, Connecticut. They were regarded as moderates, appointed because of their reputation for affability and popularity with their fellow bishops, as well as their nonideological perspective. Then there were two bishops with strongly opposing attitudes: Gumbleton, the well-known pacifist, and Bishop John O'Connor, then a bishop assigned to the military vicariate, who would later become the archbishop of New York.

Gumbleton didn't expect much support for the pacifist position from his fellow bishops in the conference. But there were a few bishops who strongly advocated for an uncompromising rejection of nuclear weapons. Chief among these was Gumbleton's friend and ally Archbishop Raymond Hunthausen of Seattle. Hunthausen had attracted national attention for his protests against the Trident submarine, a vital part of the U.S. nuclear arsenal, which was based in the Seattle area.[2] Hunthausen said these nuclear weapons in the blue waters of his city

2. John A. McCoy, *A Still and Quiet Conscience: The Archbishop Who Challenged a Pope, a President, and a Church* (Maryknoll, NY: Orbis Books, 2015).

represented "the Auschwitz of Puget Sound." As a sign of his opposition, he had vowed to withhold a portion of his federal income taxes in protest. But much of the bishops' conference was far removed from that position.

At the opposite end of the spectrum was John O'Connor, then in his early sixties, a long-time naval chaplain. He had a reputation for loyalty, both to his superiors in the church and in the military, where he had risen to the rank of admiral. Pacifists like Gumbleton viewed the military vicariate with a certain suspicion. Their questions didn't arise over routine pastoral ministry, whether offering the sacraments or counseling families stressed by long deployments. But when thrust into contentious conflicts such as Vietnam, military chaplains were often seen as apologists for U.S. foreign and military policy. Chaplains themselves were officers, beholden to the chain of command, as well as loyal to the church. How could they effectively serve two masters? That was the question that antiwar activists frequently raised.

O'Connor had himself written a stirring defense of American involvement in Vietnam (a book he later disavowed). When it came to discussions about the roots of U.S. deterrence policy, O'Connor could be counted on to make the case that nuclear weapons were a necessary evil in preserving the peace.

As far as the public was concerned, the main focus was on Gumbleton and O'Connor. One observer noted that whoever had put them together—whether Roach or Bernardin—had either a great sense of humor or a strategic purpose. Probably it was the latter. If those two could agree on a statement, it was thought, it would be easy to sell it to the wider body of bishops.

The committee met with a wide range of witnesses, including scholars, committed peace activists, as well as government officials. Among the latter was Caspar Weinberger, then-secretary of defense in the Reagan administration. They met at the Pentagon, with the very busy director of the world's largest military offering the bishops an entire afternoon devoted to the

U.S. defense posture. Gumbleton got to what he thought was the nub of the matter. He asked if the government ever contemplated nuclear annihilation if the United States was attacked.

Weinberger said that response was part of the U.S. strategy. It was well known. Risking world destruction was a central pillar of the U.S. defense strategy. For Gumbleton, this was more than simply stating the obvious. He found the blunt response deeply shocking. What to many seemed like common sense, Gumbleton saw as an abomination, an affront to any Christian principle.

Decades later in a column on the *NCR* website in 2017, Gumbleton described that response as indicative of "a sin beyond belief, beyond comprehension. It's not the way of Jesus. It's not the way of the Gospels. Yet, it goes on and we don't protest. We don't find some ways to try to change that policy of our nation."[3] Yet that policy was the reality, as it still is. How to deal with that reality, and whether it was a moral response to a dangerous world situation, was the question for the committee. Could this stance in favor of mutually assured destruction be something that Catholics should tolerate?

Discussions continued with the committee. Bernardin, always the reconciler, would bring the five bishops together. Bernardin's approach was to hear all views, and then find a place where everyone could agree. The Chicago archbishop was a master at smoothing over disparate views, even those as far apart as O'Connor's and Gumbleton's. The hope was that there was a point, in Catholic tradition, where the bishops would be able to come together.

The committee was joined in its work by the able Father Bryan Hehir, a Boston priest who had once studied under Henry Kissinger at Harvard, and who was placed in charge of thrashing out the wording. And ultimately, they would come to an agreement that they could all accept. The stakes were high

3. Thomas Gumbleton, "Try to Follow God's Ways, Not Our Ways," The Peace Pulpit, *National Catholic Reporter*, September 28, 2017.

and they all knew it—nothing less than the very future of the planet. Committee drafting meetings were a laborious process. Sentences and phrases were parsed in talmudic detail. As the slog continued, a consensus would often seem to emerge. But just as often, when it seemed that they had reached an agreement on some point, O'Connor had the habit of revisiting the question at the next meeting. To Gumbleton, it was obvious that his fellow committee member was taking the passages and running them by his military colleagues.

The military and the administration, said Gumbleton, "were very wary of what we were going to say." Input from the arms experts in the administration was solicited and largely provided. Getting input from experts was a new strand of development in church documents, which previously had largely relied on theologians producing products largely in isolation. The views of those who knew about and implemented policy were needed to make the document speak credibly to the wider world, which was directed not only at Catholics but at anyone with an inclination to use reason and justice to forge a better world.

Weinberger, for one, understood the stakes involved and was willing to give time to the group. He had long served in Republican politics. A former cabinet official under Richard Nixon, he was now in charge of the largest military arsenal ever accumulated. He enthusiastically applied himself to one of Reagan's key goals, to outpace the Soviets in the Cold War. The sticking point was the issue of deterrence. The bishops wondered if it was moral to threaten what church teaching, evolving from Vatican II and Pope John's *Pacem in Terris,* specifically forbade, namely, the direct massive killing of civilians. That teaching was frequently cited as the only condemnation issued by the council.

"Was it just a bluff?" Weinberger was asked by the Detroit auxiliary bishop. "Or is it for real?" As Gumbleton remembered it, Weinberger was remarkably unwilling to smooth over ugly realities for a group of religious leaders. "When we have to, we will," he responded. In other words, there were no moral qualms about preparing for mutually assured destruction, the defense doctrine that undergirded American policy in the Cold War. "To me that made it clear that deterrence was wrong," Gumbleton recalled.

Gumbleton looked for answers in the response of other conservative leaders. General George Lee Butler, the former head of the Strategic Air Command, had in retirement become an outspoken advocate for nuclear disarmament, fearful of the impact of the weapons he once administered to as part of the chain of command. Cardinal John Krol of Philadelphia, though known for his conservative and traditional views, and, as an American of Polish background, quite wary of Soviet aggression, was still quite clear that it was immoral to threaten what it was not moral to do. "For me the moral question is the intention," said Gumbleton. Jesus noted that lusting in one's heart is morally akin to actual adultery. "It's clear moral theology. Once you have the intention to do it you have already committed a sin."

As they began to accept that logic, the bishops' committee was moving toward a groundbreaking document that would question the entire basis of U.S. nuclear deterrence. It would begin the process of possibly moving the Catholic Church in the direction of "peace churches" like the Quakers or Mennonites, which had always rejected violence in implementing foreign policy goals. This would also put the church into conflict with a popular administration and its top priority, winning the Cold War. How would Catholics respond to such a stirring, prophetic document? What about the hundreds of thousands of American Catholics serving in the military? How would they be affected? How would ordinary Catholic voters respond? Could Catholic taxpayers continue to support a defense strategy that their church leaders described as inherently immoral?

But the committee was soon told to apply the brakes. "Someone from the government got to the pope," recalled Gumbleton. John Paul II, at the time immersed in support for the freedom movements in Eastern Europe, particularly his native Poland, had forged an implicit alliance with the Reagan administration, and needed American support. The stakes were indeed high. Given the influence of the United States, this statement would be seen as a universal church document, not just a view of a group of local bishops. At the same time, the bishops in France and Germany, among the countries uncomfortably close to the front lines of Soviet domination, were also wary.

Bernardin was called to Rome. The result was that the pope's concerns found their way into the final document. It offered a middle ground to the knotty question of nuclear deterrence. It was morally permissible, the document said, for governments to continue nuclear deterrence, threatening to blow up the world, as long as this was considered an interim step on the way to ultimate disarmament.

The final product was a pastoral letter titled "The Challenge of Peace: God's Promise and Our Response." It was overwhelmingly approved by the bishops' conference, becoming part of official church teaching on the subject. Bernardin had successfully shepherded a process that produced consensus, even if it had backed away from a direct challenge to U.S. military policy.

The final document offered four moral judgments. The first three points were (1) that the use of nuclear weapons could not be morally justified; (2) that battlefield use was also ruled out for its potential to escalate conflicts; and (3) that nuclear weapons could not be used for vengeance or retaliation. The fourth issue, their use as a deterrence, was accepted, in the John Paul II formula, as a temporary measure.[4]

The bishops were credited with creating a substantial reflection on an issue that was beginning to fray public discourse. But Gumbleton, the sole pacifist voice on the panel, came away disappointed. The wording called for a conditioned moral acceptance of nuclear deterrence. In other words, the policy

---

4. "The Challenge of Peace: God's Promise and Our Response," National Conference of Catholic Bishops, May 3, 1983, www.usccb.org.

of threatened mass destruction, the concept behind America's nuclear arsenal, was morally sanctioned if the long-term goal of nuclear disarmament was kept as a goal. Weinberger's view, in other words, was morally sanctioned, as long as it was seen as part of an overall process, not an end goal. When would the question be revisited? That would remain a dangling question, as the bishops in later years would move on from the issue. For Gumbleton, it was the best he could get, considering O'Connor's lobbying efforts and the Vatican's clear messages to Bernardin. He voted to support the committee's final document.

For years afterward, the Detroit auxiliary would beseech his fellow bishops to revisit the issue, to declare that nuclear weapons had long passed from being a temporary solution and had become a deadly permanent fixture in the Cold War and beyond. He could never generate enough support within the conference, however. With the pastoral letter on peace, followed by a subsequent pastoral letter on the U.S. economy, the days when the U.S. bishops could come together and address long-term difficult political and social issues soon became only a memory. By and large, they turned their attention more in the direction of internal church issues.

Gumbleton's friend, Archbishop Hunthausen from Seattle, never wavered. Hunthausen argued that deterrence was wrong and could never be conditioned by the caveat that it was a temporary, limited action. "He never gave in," Gumbleton recalled years later, about a year after Hunthausen's death in 2018. "I always regretted that I didn't stick with him."[5]

In retrospect, looking at the pastoral from the perspective of 2018, Gumbleton worried that the bishops didn't go far enough. The time to break away from the moral conditions of keeping nuclear weapons had, in Gumbleton's view, long since passed. Thirty-five years after "The Challenge of Peace," even long after the supposed end of the Cold War, the superpowers still

---

5. Interview with Bishop Thomas Gumbleton, June 2018.

maintained their nuclear stockpiles. Other countries had their own arsenals, or sought to obtain them. The world continued to exist under the canopy of nuclear catastrophe. When Joshua McElwee of *National Catholic Reporter* interviewed Gumbleton in December 2017, the bishop expressed a desire that the church in the United States more closely follow Pope Francis's lead. In 2017, the pope argued that the very possession of nuclear weapons should be condemned, the very argument that Gumbleton had put forth in 1983. Papal teaching was moving in Gumbleton's direction. "That means we have to disarm," said Gumbleton. "And the United States obviously, since we have the largest capability of nuclear destruction, we should be in the front row of those trying to change things."[6]

The goal of ultimate nuclear disarmament remained elusive. In the era of President Donald Trump the stated goal of his administration remained strategic dominance, not disarmament. The bishops had no real commitment to follow up on evaluating the deterrence strategy. They never revisited the 1983 document. In retrospect, said Gumbleton, he regretted his inclination to compromise.

---

6. Joshua McElwee, "Gumbleton on Nuclear Deterrence," *National Catholic Reporter*, November 22, 2017.

Chapter 8

A Mother's Question

"Is Dan going to hell?"

Ever since his outspoken opposition to the Vietnam War, Gumbleton had assumed an unofficial role as a kind of chaplain for social and peace activists around the world, whether Catholic or not. In 1972 he helped to solidify that legacy through his work with Bishop Carroll Dozier of Memphis and other Catholic peace activists, including Eileen Egan and Gordon Zahn, in establishing Pax Christi USA. This was an American branch of the international Pax Christi organization founded in Europe among French Catholics after World War II. With its message of peace and reconciliation, Pax Christi was seen as an influence on the evolving teachings on peace in the Catholic Church that reached fruition with Popes John XXIII and Paul VI, as well as the Vatican Council's condemnation of nuclear war.[1]

As the founding president of Pax Christi USA, and for many years one of its "Ambassadors of Peace," Gumbleton undertook extensive travels throughout the world. In Europe, he supported the canonization efforts for Franz Jägerstätter, the Austrian Catholic who was beheaded for refusing induction in the Nazi army. He made frequent trips to Haiti, where he became

1. Bill McSweeney, "Bishop Gumbleton and Pax Christi USA's Priorities," *National Catholic Reporter*, August 24, 1990.

a prominent supporter of Jean-Bertrand Aristide, a Catholic priest and proponent of liberation theology, who was elected president after the downfall of the long-running Duvalier dictatorship.

Still, even when Gumbleton traveled in his later years, he almost always returned to St. Leo's Church for Sunday Mass. The parish remained his spiritual bulwark.

His friends would say that the bishop was a natural introvert. His approach to issues was to listen, ask questions, seek advice, and place himself in situations where people were struggling. "He wanted to be in places where it was all about economic justice," said Father Norman Thomas.[2]

Much of his ministry was outside the gaze of the media, including visits to Michigan prisons and his support for a medical mission in Haiti. On his eightieth birthday, during a visit to earthquake-ravaged Haiti, Gumbleton slept in the open air alongside Haitians made homeless by the disaster.

"I don't think there is any other bishop who would do that," said Benedictine Sister Anne McCarthy, a former staffer at Pax Christi USA who worked with Gumbleton, traveling with him on many overseas trips, including delegations to Central America during the height of tensions there in the 1980s.[3] "He epitomized the best of the Catholic tradition," said McCarthy. Still, she said, "when push came to shove, he would always go for the gospel over the institution."

When the federal government in the 1980s mandated that all employers seek proof that new employees were U.S. citizens or legally eligible to work in the country, Gumbleton thought Pax Christi should abstain from that requirement, believing that would compel a Catholic organization to enforce unfair immigration laws. "That was quite a risky thing for an organization to do. You could feel the full weight of the IRS," said

---

2. Norman Thomas, phone interview with author, 2017.
3. Anne McCarthy, phone interview with author, 2017.

McCarthy. Gumbleton's response was that Pax Christi could always rebuild its mailing list if it was forced to shutter. The organization declined to follow the federal regulations. It has remained in business.

While participating in his role as president of Pax Christi USA, Gumbleton marched at a United Nations' disarmament meeting in New York during the 1980s. The march was to end with a Mass, with Benedictine Sister Mary Lou Kownacki as the featured homilist. This raised the concern of now-Cardinal John J. O'Connor, who called up Gumbleton, noting that church regulations forbade nonordained persons from preaching at Mass. Some saw the rule as a way to assure that women did not ascend to the pulpit in Catholic parishes. At first, Gumbleton promised to go along, telling the Pax Christi activists that they needed to follow the cardinal's dictates for the greater good of the antinuclear weapons movement. But when the time came, Gumbleton pointed Kownacki toward the pulpit, urging her to deliver the homily. It was an indication, said McCarthy, that Gumbleton was reluctant to cooperate with what he saw as injustice, even when it involved church regulations. It was an unusual stance for a bishop to take, one of many for which he would take heat in the conservative Catholic press. Nevertheless, "He wasn't afraid of being criticized," his old friend Sister Suzanne Sattler, noted. "He didn't want to be simply affirmed."[4]

For McCarthy, Gumbleton was a mix of church tradition and contemporary social activism. "His upbringing was steeped in the Catholic ghetto. That was his strength. He was in the Catholic tradition. But what he did with that tradition took him to a new age."

Perhaps that engagement with Catholic tradition, combined with an opening to reading the signs of the times, was never more challenged than when Gumbleton became involved in speaking out for the rights of gay and lesbian Catholics. It all

4. Suzanne Sattler, phone interview with author, 2017.

went back to a simple invitation to a wedding, which Gumbleton remembers as taking place in the early 1990s. The invitation was for the wedding of Gumbleton's niece, the daughter of his younger brother Dan, who had moved with his wife and four children from Michigan to California decades before. Dan was a social worker who did family counseling. With the invitation was a letter. Dan, anticipating a crowded family venue, wanted to let everyone else in on his personal circumstances, so there would be no awkward disclosures. He was gay. He would be attending his daughter's wedding with his partner, Carl.[5]

If the letter sent shock waves through the Gumbleton family, it wasn't immediately apparent. Bishop Gumbleton didn't say a word to anyone—not to his siblings, nor to his mother (now a widow, following the death of her husband, Vincent, in 1976). Still, they all went out for the wedding. The Gumbleton family members remained tight lipped. They all liked Carl, and the wedding went off without a hitch. "We came back home and no one said anything. It's kind of Irish where we don't communicate very well," Gumbleton remembered. If there was any intrafamily communication about the matter, the family bishop was left entirely out of the loop. Perhaps they hadn't wanted to draw him into an issue with wider church implications.

In fact, the bishop had never thought too much about homosexuality. During his time in Dearborn, he would often hear confessions from guilt-ridden gays and lesbians. He would tell them not to sin again, to avoid places where temptation might lurk, but otherwise he had little to offer. What he had learned in seminary was clear: homosexuality was a sin that people deliberately chose. "That was no help at all," Gumbleton recalled about his confession advice. "I had no pastoral way of dealing with it. I told them to do the best you can and gave them absolution. I don't think I convinced anyone."

Now the issue was presenting itself within his own family. Upon his return from California, Gumbleton began exploring

5. Bishop Gumbleton, interview with author, December 2018.

the topic. He knew from his seminary training that the general belief was that gays chose this particular kind of life, that it was a conscious sin, that it could be overcome with enough prayer and support and sometimes, as his brother attempted, through entering into a heterosexual marriage. In its cruder forms this approach would later be referred to as "praying away the gay."

But what Gumbleton read began to indicate more complexity. An article by Andrew Sullivan in *America* magazine, a Jesuit publication, offered a plea for the church to welcome gay and lesbian Catholics.[6] Gumbleton would later quote Sullivan at events sponsored by New Ways Ministry, a group devoted to LGBT Catholics and their families in the church. Gumbleton became one of the few bishops to attend their conferences.

Gumbleton had moved from international peace activist and defender of the poor in Detroit into a realm where church teaching itself posed more of an obstacle. He was castigated in much of the conservative Catholic press for violating Catholic doctrine.

Like other bishops supportive of a new approach to the question, Gumbleton steered away from endorsing homosexual acts. That would put him directly at odds with church teaching. But church teaching also encouraged Catholics to treat LGBT people with dignity and respect, a portion of the teaching that came naturally, ever since his brother Dan had come out of the closet for that California wedding. It was a story he would regularly repeat on the Catholic lecture circuit.

Gumbleton made a regular point of visiting the family home, now in the Detroit suburbs, as he traveled the archdiocese. His mother would make him dinner, and he could catch up on family news. It was a habit he maintained ever since his ordination and his days working in the chancery. The family home had become a sanctuary, a place away from the rush of church business.

---

6. Thomas Stahel, "I'm Here: An Interview with Andrew Sullivan," *America*, May 8, 1993.

Months after Dan's stunning announcement, his mother on one of those visits broached the topic for the first time. The family had remained silent. But she had a direct question for her bishop son: "Is Dan going to hell?" she asked. His studies on the topic made Gumbleton assured that the answer to that question was a resounding no. "This had been weighing on her. She was going through agony," he recalled. "But by that time I had learned something. . . . I was able to reassure my mother right away," he said. As he left the house that day, he began to think about similar conversations going on in Catholic households all over the country. There must be many parents dealing with concern for their gay children.

He made a point of contacting Cardinal Joseph Bernardin, with whom he had worked closely on the pastoral letter on nuclear weapons. Bernardin had since been appointed to serve as head of the bishops' committee on family issues. Gumbleton suggested that the bishops put out a pastoral letter directed to parents of gay children. His mother's question would be answered, this time writ large. Bernardin agreed.

The result: In 1994, the U.S. bishops issued "Always Our Children," a landmark in the church's view of homosexuality.[7] The document avoided the most contentious issues. Instead, it urged parents to support their gay children, not to drum them out of family life. It emphasized God's mercy and promised support from the church for parents dealing with these difficult questions. The document noted that the causes of homosexuality were complex and could not be placed on the shoulders of indifferent fathers or overly involved mothers. It said that homosexuality could often not be considered a conscious choice.

Its welcoming tone was criticized in much of the conservative Catholic press. Gay activists thought the pastoral did not go

---

7. "Always Our Children: A Pastoral Message to Parents of Homosexual Children and Suggestions for Pastoral Ministers," www.usccb.org.

far enough in sanctioning gay relationships. But unlike his reservations with the final results of the peace pastoral, this time Gumbleton was pleased, seeing it as a step forward.

"It was a pretty good letter," he said. "It made it clear that homosexuality was not a choice." He heard from parents around the country who praised it for affirming their own struggles. It was not a document that garnered the giant reaction of "The Challenge of Peace." It was more directed to a particular group of Catholics. Ultimately it was an answer to the question raised by Gumbleton's mother about her son Dan. The response from parents of gay Catholics was overwhelmingly positive. The bishops were praised for a pastoral response to a sensitive issue.

That period of warm feelings, however, was not to last. The initial version, facing criticism from a resurgent traditionalist wing in the church, was later revised. Another version was issued three years later, this time omitting the portion that denied homosexuality was a conscious choice.

Meanwhile, Cardinal Joseph Ratzinger, head of the Congregation of the Doctrine of the Faith in the Vatican and who was later to become Pope Benedict XVI, issued a document that described homosexuals as "intrinsically disordered."[8] For Gumbleton, the combination of these two statements was a case of one step forward, another step back. For many gay Catholics, the language of "intrinsically disordered" was deeply hurtful.

As the wider church argued over the impact of gay rights, Gumbleton spoke regularly at conferences for gay Catholics. Rare for the bishop, Gumbleton began to invoke personal family stories. His mother's reaction was a prime subject.

At one 1997 meeting in Winnipeg, Canada, Gumbleton argued that church teaching lacked direction and guidance for gay people. "We have done nothing to help these people discover the divine purpose for their homosexuality," he said during a retreat in the Canadian city. "We have to do more than tell

8. Peter Steinfels, "Bishops Protest Vatican Advisory Citing Anti-Homosexual Bias," *New York Times*, November 2, 1992, B11.

them that they are acceptable as long as they are celibate. Does the gift of celibacy automatically come with homosexuality?" he asked. "If the gift of celibacy for priests and religious is given for the benefit of their particular ministries, for what particular purpose is the church expecting the same of gay and lesbian people?"[9] Phrasing the discussion in the form of questions indicated a willingness to be more open, while at the same time not directly attacking church teaching.

As groups such as New Ways Ministry came under increasing attack from many bishops, Vatican officials, and traditionalists, Gumbleton remained one of the few bishops who would attend and speak at their conferences. At one such meeting in Chicago in 1992, Gumbleton was joined by his friend, Bishop Ken Untener, then-bishop of Saginaw, Michigan, and a former Detroit priest, and Bishop William Hughes of Covington, Kentucky. It was a time when church heavyweights such as Cardinal John J. O'Connor in New York and Cardinal Bernard Law in Boston were holding fast to a call for gay Catholics to remain celibate. Meanwhile, the raging AIDS pandemic had intensified the anger of many gay activists at the institutional church. One militant group, ACT UP, protesting the church's opposition to safe sex education and the distribution of condoms, had disrupted a Mass in St. Patrick's Cathedral. There was intense animosity on both sides, often flaring when church officials opposed civil rights legislation on behalf of gay people, legislation the church frequently perceived as a sanction for immoral behavior.

Gumbleton acknowledged that many in the church were unhappy with his presence at the New Ways conference. "I have to be careful what I say," he told the meeting. As usual, in many ways, he often was at least perceived as throwing caution to the wind. Even without saying too much, his very presence spoke volumes. Gumbleton invoked Catholic tradition in explaining his views. From Cardinal Newman in the nineteenth century to Vatican II, the teaching was that Catholics were obligated to

9. Dorothy Lachance, *Prairie Messenger*, April 23, 1997.

follow their conscience, with the caveat that their conscience be well formed.

Gumbleton conveyed that message to gay audiences and their supporters: "Listen to the voice deep in your heart," he said. Then consult the Scriptures, Catholic tradition and a spiritual guide. What emerged from that painstaking struggle—it was not supposed to be easy—was that you were obligated to follow it. There was no other alternative. "You can't violate your conscience," he said.[10]

By the early 1990s, Gumbleton pushed the view that priests who were gay should come out of the closet, much as his brother Dan had done. By staying closeted, gay priests were guilty of letting other LGBT people become victimized, unknown as people working as ministers and serving the church. Such a move, he said, would "more quickly than anything else put down a lot of myths and stereotypes."[11] Few took him up on the offer, even as the number of gay priests, according to studies by researchers such as Richard Sipe, continued to far outpace the percentage of gays in other professions.

It would take another few decades before that focus of Catholic teaching gained further support with the emergence of Pope Francis. There was a more open spirit in the papacy. "Who am I to judge?" Francis famously asked, setting off headlines around the world in a new social media age. In his visit to the United States, Francis hosted a former gay student and his spouse. The church was now more formally focused on respecting the dignity of all.

Gumbleton, for one, had always been there. A New Ways Ministry newsletter noted that "when the history of LGBT issues in the Catholic Church gets written, a large chapter (or maybe several) will have to be devoted to Bishop Thomas Gumbleton."[12]

---

10. Interview with Bishop Thomas Gumbleton, June 2018.
11. Ibid.
12. "Bishop Gumbleton's Tour of LGBT Listening Sessions," New Ways Ministry Bondings 2.0 newsletter, November 25, 2017.

In a 1994 visit to Minnesota's Twin Cities, the *National Catholic Reporter* noted how Gumbleton conducted a listening tour for gay ministry.[13] The bishop rarely wore his miter, but for this trip he did, except it contained a pink triangle, cross, and rainbow ribbon. *NCR* reporter Dawn Gibeau commented: "The three days and five forums during which a bishop listened and talked appear to be unprecedented in this nation or any other."[14]

Gumbleton was willing to embrace the message of "Always Our Children," the pastoral letter he urged the bishops to write and which they passed in 1997. Four words were striking in the message of that document. It urged church pastoral ministers to take up a simple bit of advice: "Strive first to listen."

Gay rights became a regular cause for the auxiliary bishop. As such rights became more widely accepted, activists began to promote legal solutions to long-term issues of discrimination. Often, that took the form of state referendums to extend civil rights protections for LGBT people in jobs, housing, and marriage privileges. Michigan became a focal point. Gumbleton would frequently find himself a lone voice among the state's bishops.

After the U.S. Supreme Court ruled in favor of marriage equality in 2015, the Michigan bishops argued that the ruling would "create inestimable conflicts between the state" and the church. Marriage, according to church teaching, should remain between a man and a woman, the bishops stated.[15]

At the same time, reflecting the conundrum faced by Catholic leaders, the bishops recognized the need for all to be treated with care and compassion. "The experience of same-sex attrac-

---

13. Ken Chandler, "Bishop Says Church Is Negligent on Gay Rights," *Minneapolis Star Tribune*, B02, October 28, 1994.

14. Dawn Gibeau, "Gumbleton Hears Gay Stories, Some Angry," *National Catholic Reporter*, November 11, 1994.

15. Patricia Montemurri, "Ruling Creates Inestimable Conflicts," *Detroit Free Press*, June 26, 2015.

tion is a reality that calls for attention, sensitivity and pastoral care," they said.[16]

Gumbleton, of course, was not among the bishops who signed on to the statement. Press accounts noted that the Michigan bishops had spent more than a million dollars to support what turned out to be an unsuccessful effort in 2004 to ban same-sex marriage in the state's constitution.

In 2014, Archbishop Allen Henry Vigneron of Detroit questioned whether Catholics who supported same-sex marriage should be allowed to receive Communion.[17]

Gumbleton, while his fellow bishops were decrying the Supreme Court ruling, urged them to reflect. He suggested they spend their resources on other issues and allow the civic order to continue its extension of gay rights without further church opposition. "They should not get into a panic that this is going to destroy all of society," Gumbleton said.[18] He suggested that the Michigan bishops follow the lead of Pope Francis, famous for asking "Who am I to judge?" when confronted with the case of a gay priest. The pope had cautioned bishops not to focus so much on divisive culture war issues.

As usual, Gumbleton couldn't help but comment on other issues, questioning whether bishops should put so much moral and financial capital on regulating gay rights. "We have every right to teach and we have every right to convince people to follow our teaching," he said. "But we don't have the right to impose it on them."[19]

He reminded the bishops that they should focus their energies on other concerns, such as nuclear weapons. "There are more moral issues than just one to oppose," he said.[20] Seven years after he had lost his parish after questioning his fellow

---

16. Ibid.

17. Niraj Warikoo, "Catholic Leaders Speak Out against Same-Sex Relationships," *Detroit Free Press*, August 13, 2015.

18. Interview with Bishop Thomas Gumbleton, June 2018.

19. Ibid.

20. Ibid.

bishops about the sex abuse statute of limitations, and well into his eighties, Gumbleton was still speaking out.

Homosexuality was not the only internal church issue that Gumbleton was ready to go out on a limb about. While his forays into political activism raised hackles, for many traditional Catholics it was issues where he was seen to be arguing against the pope and church tradition where Gumbleton faced the most severe criticism. The social justice and peace issues had solid backing in church documents; other issues, pertaining to how the church ran its business, far less.

Among these issues was women's ordination. Gumbleton joined a small group, including his friend Bishop Kenneth Untener, Bishop Raymond Lucker of the Diocese of New Ulm, Minnesota, and Francis Murphy, Baltimore auxiliary, who argued that the church should continue to engage the issue, even after Pope John Paul II had long closed the door shut. That pope's statement was supposed to be definitive, telling the world that the church was bound by the teachings of the gospel to reserve the clerical role for men, based on the tradition that Jesus had selected only men among his twelve apostles. Gumbleton was more reserved after that statement, not willing to be in open defiance, although he continued to speak to women's groups and others who saw the signs of the times and the growth of feminism as a reason to expand the church's definition. Still, the issue in internal church circles took a back seat, while others emerged more strongly.

Differences in the church often reflected different interpretations of the significance and ongoing meaning of Vatican II. There were those like Pope John Paul II and Benedict XVI who saw the council as a continuation of previous church teaching, not a mandate to go beyond what the documents had already prescribed. Others, including Gumbleton, invoked what they saw as a spirit of the council that could be used to push the church further along the path of reform.

Dearden, for one, had proved to be a vital link to the council. He came home possessed by the sense that the church needed to change and was open to discussion and conferences that were unafraid to raise sensitive issues. Detroit became the host of what became known as the Call to Action Conference, starting in 1976, which called for changes across the board, including the possibility of women's ordination and a married clergy. Other bishops returned from the council, having dipped their toes into the bracing waters of church reform, and found it too much. Dearden, in contrast, was invigorated by the entire event. He set about moving the Archdiocese of Detroit quickly along the path of renewal and speaking out aggressively on issues such as economic and racial justice.

Gumbleton, then working in chancery administration, was in the middle of organizing meetings and committees. Thousands got involved. "There was a lot of excitement in the air," he recalled. He began to seek out ways to connect with the changes he knew were coming to the church. To make sense of it all and to recharge his spiritual batteries, he sought out retreats led by a Jesuit, Howard Gray. Gray, who died in 2018, drew on the wisdom of Jesuit spirituality. Drawing on the methods of St. Ignatius of Loyola, the Jesuit founder and author of *The Spiritual Exercises*, he encouraged retreatants to put themselves into a gospel story. In the parable of the Prodigal Son, for example, retreatants were asked about whom they related to more. The forgiving father? The sinful son? Or the "good" son, who had done his father's bidding and resented the outpouring of support and love for his wayward brother who had squandered his inheritance?[21]

Or, how do you look upon the story in the Gospel of John in which Jesus is described as weeping over the death of his friend Lazarus?

The style of looking at the Bible in that way influenced Gumbleton's preaching style and his personal spirituality. He would often cite biblical parables and stories as a way to explain

---

21. Peter Feuerherd, "Fr. Howard Gray, Ignatian Spirituality Scholar, Dies after Car Accident," *National Catholic Reporter*, May 8, 2018.

his social justice outlook, whether that meant fighting Detroit church closings, Central American dictators, or nuclear war policies.

His critics tended to see Gumbleton's political activism as a gospel add-on. They saw the core of his beliefs in the peace and civil rights actions, with the Scriptures simply a justifying device for firmly held social and political views. But for Gumbleton there was no such rupture. It was all of one piece. The Scriptures called him to be active; the ways of living that out were about discernment, but deep down there was no real alternative. Conscience called and the auxiliary bishop of Detroit answered.

In 1994 Bishop Gumbleton wears a miter adorned with rainbow colors for a "eucharistic liturgy of liberation" at the Basilica of St. Mary in Minneapolis, followed by a listening session for LGBT Catholics. Credit: Courtesy Thomas Gumbleton

Chapter 9

A Legacy of Persistence

"We all probably experience God taking our lives in a different direction than we ever imagined."

Why write about a bishop in today's church? The answer, regarding Gumbleton, could be seen in the example of his life, as well as the words he preached. Both had something profound to say about what real religious authority can be.

As the winter of 2019 approached, Gumbleton had moved from St. Leo's Church to an office above his living quarters on Bagley Street, a few blocks from the site of the old Tiger Stadium where he used to usher as a teenager.

It is a modest office atop his modest living quarters in what is called Corktown, Detroit's traditionally Irish neighborhood, a place where the Irish largely left, to be replaced by Latinos and African Americans. Now the neighborhood is going through another change, with condos at the site of the old ballpark going for $400,000, a shock for old-time Detroiters like the bishop, who are accustomed to the idea that the Motor City is largely immune to the ebbs and flows of the real estate market.

Unlike his old office at St. Leo's, the desk in Corktown is filled with memorabilia accumulated over eight decades. Perched on Gumbleton's desk are personal photos and mementos: a portrait of Franziska Jägerstätter, the widow of Franz Jägerstätter, the Austrian Catholic who was executed by the Nazis for oppos-

Bishop Gumbleton with Franziska Jägerstätter, whose husband, Franz, was martyred under the Nazis (and later beatified). Credit: Courtesy Thomas Gumbleton

ing the Third Reich; the funeral program for Barbara Blaine, sex abuse survivor and activist; an aerial shot of the old Tiger Stadium, and the funeral program for Father Clement Kern, a Detroit priest who became known for his devotion to labor struggles and was one of Gumbleton's city pastor colleagues. On the other side of the desk are photos of other saintly figures dedicated to peace and service to the poor: Father Dan Berrigan, the famous Jesuit activist, and Father Solanus Casey, the Capuchin priest beatified for his work among the poor of Detroit and New York. The archdiocese had orchestrated a giant beatification event for Father Casey, filling Ford Field with some seventy thousand devoted Catholics, a sign that the church could still generate a crowd when the circumstances were right.

Gumbleton was now close to his eighty-ninth birthday. He no longer participated in acts of civil disobedience. In his retirement years, Gumbleton's activism continued, but at a different pace, with a new set of strategies. His frustration with church leadership had become increasingly pronounced. In 2007, he was honored with Voice of the Faithful's "Priest of Integrity Award." Voice of the Faithful grew out of the 2002 Boston Archdiocese sex abuse scandals with the view that the church could be rescued by involved lay people.

Gumbleton told the group their search for renewed church leadership was a difficult one. "What has happened in the last thirty years is that the criteria for naming bishops . . . almost inevitably brings forward priests who are not genuine leaders," he said. The key test remained loyalty. The end result was mediocrity. "So you begin to get a structure where everything comes from the top and works its way down, so you don't get people who have initiative, who have imagination, who are creative, who are the type of people you need as leaders."[1] "Leaders are not people who simply conform to what somebody else tells them," he said. Was he talking about himself?

At that occasion, Gumbleton was seventy-seven, far removed from the corridors of church power. It was a year since his testimony in front of the Ohio legislature and his removal as pastor at St. Leo's. He frequently noted that bishops were prone to put forward as new bishops those who would not outshine them. One could see some nostalgia for the days of Dearden, a leader who let his subordinates shine and develop the kind of activism which, by 2007, was largely unheard of in the church hierarchy.

Still, Gumbleton was undeterred. He kept plowing along, seeking spots where a little grass-roots activism could be effective. One such opportunity arose with what became known as the Elephants in the Living Room Group, named for a pop psychology insight about how troubled families often overlook glaring trouble in their midst. The analogy was applied to the church and, in particular, the Archdiocese of Detroit. The goal, said Gumbleton, was "to talk about issues that confront the

1. Joe Feuerherd, "Gumbleton Decries Lack of Leaders," *National Catholic Reporter*, March 16, 2007.

church, issues that they won't talk about." The gathering grew out of the experience of a group of Detroit priests, frustrated with Cardinal Adam Maida's unwillingness to talk about the lingering crisis of how to staff parishes with fewer and fewer priests. They decided to talk about it on their own, naming the elephant in the room that they felt Maida declined to recognize. Joined by interested lay people, they sponsored a series of lectures addressing church issues, about six or seven times a year. Occasionally the archdiocese would decline them access to Catholic property to hold the talks, especially when they invited theologians who were involved in controversy, such as Sister Elizabeth Johnson or Father Charles Curran.[2]

The Elephants Group became more active as the turbulent 2018 year enveloped the church in the United States. It had been a horrific summer for the church in the United States, and as fall began its decline into winter seemingly little had changed. The scandals surrounding Cardinal Theodore McCarrick and the Pennsylvania grand jury report made the headlines, and the U.S. bishops, just off their annual November meeting, were being enjoined by Pope Francis from taking any action prior to a Vatican-planned worldwide conference in February 2019. The idea of waiting was not a popular one, either with traditionalists or liberal reformers alike. Both sides were quite willing to use the crisis as a way of reaffirming points about the church. For traditionalists, the issue was the growth of a gay clergy. For liberal reformers, the issue was clericalism, the attitude of priests who acted like princes in the church and felt entitled to protection and support. Gumbleton, for one, didn't know about McCarrick's proclivities. But ever since the 1990s, Gumbleton had grown increasingly disillusioned with the wider body of bishops. He no longer felt it was valuable to attend the annual meetings. Gumbleton at one time had been a force, albeit that of a minority view among the bishops. His involvement with the "Challenge of Peace" pastoral was well known, and, during

2. Bishop Gumbleton, interview with author, December 2018.

Bishop Gumbleton with Paul Moore, Episcopal Bishop of New York City, at a press conference in support of peace witness in Central America. Credit: Rick Reinhard

the buildup to the first Iraq war, he had organized a group of bishops to protest the impending conflict (on that score he also had the support of John Paul II).

The bishops had come together and agreed on a statement at their meeting in November 1990. Then war came in January, two months later. As Americans watched bombers and missiles pummel Baghdad, the nation's Catholic bishops fell silent. "Not one bishop in the country made a public protest. That's how useless those statements were," recalled Gumbleton.[3]

For all his activism, most people, whether critics or supporters, tended to overlook one aspect that animated Gumbleton's life: He remained a Catholic bishop, dedicated to a spiritual practice rooted in two thousand years of tradition. Every day he prayed the Rosary, a devotional exercise focused on remembering the great events in the life of Jesus and Mary. It was a

3. Ibid.

practice that connected him to Catholics around the world, including many of the traditionalists who routinely attacked the auxiliary bishop for his statements on peace and social issues. As the years went on, Gumbleton's overt public activism took other forms than street actions. He had grown tired of civil disobedience. Such actions rarely made a media splash anymore, even when they involved a Catholic bishop. "I haven't done it in a long time," he said, a month before his eighty-ninth birthday. The burning issues remained, and, as the Trump administration began ramping up the military budget, he felt "we have to come out with a new strategy." He was still looking for ways to break through social inertia, but civil disobedience appeared to be one tactic that had passed its prime.

Gumbleton's spirituality remained evident in the long-running series of homilies he published for the *National Catholic Reporter*. Through it all rises a single theme: Getting immersed in the issues of the world, while being deeply rooted in Catholic spirituality, is not a contradiction. Both feed on each other. As he regularly points out, citing a statement of the 1971 Synod of Bishops held at the Vatican, "Action on behalf of justice is a constitutive dimension of the preaching of the Gospel."

This view took some time to take root in Gumbleton's own prayer life. The priestly training he received before Vatican II relied heavily on mastering moral and doctrinal precepts. The homilies he delivered in his early years as a parish priest were based on guidelines in a book from the chancery, delivered to all priests, that covered such themes as the Ten Commandments, the sacraments, and lessons on morality and doctrine. Spirituality focused heavily on devotional Catholicism, the Stations of the Cross and the Rosary, among other spiritual staples. But relatively little attention was paid to the Scriptures. The concept of social sin—that, for example, Catholics in Dearborn in the 1950s could be individually kind to black people but could regularly elect a racist to rule their town—was never addressed. "I thought of prayer as mostly asking, petitionary prayer," he said.

It would take a development of the wider church and Gumbleton's own life for spirituality to join the concepts of an individual's stance toward God and wider social issues. As the post–Vatican II church began looking at the wider world, so did Gumbleton in his spiritual life.

"I had to think about how my daily prayer had to be focused on transforming the world," he recalled. In the early 1970s, he began attending directed Jesuit retreats. Based on the teachings of St. Ignatius of Loyola, the Spiritual Exercises include the reading of a gospel passage followed by silent reflection. Jesuit priests undergo a thirty-day silent retreat as part of their formation; modified versions, based on a week's prayer, have been a regular staple of Catholic retreat houses. The idea is to put yourself into the story of Jesus, to reflect prayerfully on a personal reaction to the events described.

Gumbleton used the retreats as an opportunity to reflect on personal charity (the parable of the Good Samaritan), as well as the need, at times, to crash through the temple and overturn the tables of a corrupt religious and political system. All of this became a source for meditation and, later, action.

As Gumbleton reflected more on the Gospels, he found that much of his seminary training was a hindrance, not a help. The Scriptures tell the story of Jesus having friendships, both with his disciples and, unusual for his day, with women. Seminary training, in contrast, focused on avoiding "particular friendships," particularly with lay people. Even with fellow priests, friendships were viewed more as a means for recreation, rather than an opportunity to explore personal issues. In retrospect, that prohibition could be seen as an uneasiness about the potential of fostering homosexuality in the ranks of the priesthood. But it had the effect of stunting healthy human development. Church leaders who preach on behalf of the poor are often vulnerable to the charge that they themselves live far above the level of their flock. It is routine for clergy and, particularly bishops, to occupy large rectories, to

Bishop Gumbleton with retired Bishop Carroll Dozier of Memphis in 1984. Credit: *National Catholic Reporter*/Steve Askin

have their meals prepared for them, and to experience a comfortably middle-class or even affluent lifestyle. Pope Francis placed a spotlight on this by choosing to live in a modest Vatican apartment instead of the papal palace. This decision was welcomed positively throughout the world.

It was a lesson that the auxiliary bishop of Detroit had long embraced. Gumbleton was legendary for simple living. His nephew, Gerry Gumbleton, noted that his uncle made one move putting all his possessions in the back of a hatchback car.[4] When the bishop's apartment was invaded by a burglar, the thief left empty-handed, finding little of value to take, other than the photos of Dorothy Day, Oscar Romero, and other Catholic social justice heroes that lined the walls.

4. Gerry Gumbleton, phone interview with author, 2017.

"The United States has an unjust amount of wealth in the world, and we have to change that," Gumbleton once said. In his personal life, Gumbleton practiced that part of what he preached. While other bishops stayed at a high-class hotel for conferences, Gumbleton would often seek out the local YMCA.

He spoke about his ministry in an interview with Jesuit Father Sean Salai for *America* magazine in 2015, the year he reached his eighty-fifth birthday.[5] One point he made was that his priesthood had been full of surprises since being ordained in 1956.

"At some point, we all probably experience God taking our lives in a different direction than what we imagined," he said. He had expected to continue much as he had at St. Alphonsus in Dearborn, ministering in large, active parishes, one day being named a pastor. But after four years he was sent to work in chancery administration and then was brought to Rome to study for a canon law degree. Gumbleton rarely spoke about what he learned in those canon law classes. But the experience, at the cusp of the Vatican Council II gatherings, had a profound impact.

He remembered meeting theologians, such as Hans Küng and Yves Congar, who were advising bishops on the transformational changes envisioned by the council. Gumbleton was, admittedly, a bit player, just a student listening to the wisdom of his elders. "We learned just enough to be aware that extraordinary changes were happening in the church," he said.[6]

As he evolved in his priesthood, Gumbleton said he learned the value of listening. "When you come out of the seminary, you think you've got the answer to everything, but then you find out you don't. Obviously, the church was very authoritarian before the council, and to learn how to interact with people on a basis of mutuality and equality—the priest can't simply dictate things to others, but is part of a community—was a

5. Sean Salai, "Bishop Thomas Gumbleton: War Isn't the Solution to Our Problems," *America*, November 18, 2015.

6. Bishop Gumbleton, interview with author, December 2018.

challenge for me. I don't know that I've achieved that kind of mutual dialogue even today! It's something difficult for clerics and for the Catholic Church in general," he said.

In the *America* interview, he talked about how the body of bishops had changed over the years. At one point there were 140 bishops in Pax Christi USA. Now there were five. Gumbleton's comrades in support of peace and justice causes were now largely retired or deceased. There was little enthusiasm for those causes among the U.S. bishops, even during the papacy of Francis, who has reignited interest in the theme of peace and justice for the poor. While he's been a lonely voice, Gumbleton reflected, he has rarely been in real trouble with the church—the exception being with statements considered supportive of women's ordination. But what really got him in trouble, he said, was his statement on sex abuse to the Ohio legislature asking for an extension of the statute of limitations in such cases. His testimony caused his banishment from his parish.

"I knew from my own experience as a survivor that abuse is not something you can talk about easily. Within days of a complaint about my testimony, I was forced to retire as auxiliary bishop and from my post as pastor of a parish in the archdiocese. I got a letter from Rome saying I had violated the *communio episcoporum*, the 'communion of bishops.' The bishops of Ohio had spoken with one voice. My 'crime' was to offer a different perspective," he said.

During the interview, he recalled his own experience of being assaulted by a priest teacher from his high school seminary: "First of all, it wasn't that profound a trauma because I was old enough at the time to resist and get myself out of the situation. I was already fifteen when it happened, and even though I was quite innocent about sexuality, I knew what was right and wrong. I knew what was happening to me wasn't right, so I struggled against the guy and was able to stop it. So it wasn't as traumatic for me as it is for many victims who were younger and more powerless. But I knew how traumatic it could be, I counseled many victims myself, and I knew they needed pastoral care."

In his peace work, Gumbleton said his biggest frustration is the "global elephant in the room" of the ongoing possession of weapons of mass destruction in the hands of the world's great powers, as well as their potential availability to terrorist groups. "People don't seem to care about that. I just read an article complaining that Iran never lived up to the nonproliferation treaty, but neither did the United States—and that's why the world is so dangerous. When we signed that treaty, we committed ourselves under Article VI to gradually bring about mutual disarmament. But we've never made any genuine efforts in that direction. We've reduced them, but we've also made them more destructive and made the world more dangerous than ever with our 'hair-trigger alert' policy."

"Pacifism remains a tough sell," said the bishop. "We've also hung on to the mentality that war is the solution. Starting with Jesus and moving through Catholic social teaching, it's very clear that war isn't the solution to our problems. However, we haven't really taught that lesson to our people. We've never admitted or asked forgiveness for our use of nuclear weapons in Hiroshima and Nagasaki. When we say, 'that was ok' to explode an atomic bomb over Hiroshima, then all other violence looks insignificant, and we can justify just about any kind of violence. Instead of asking forgiveness for what we did, we've just looked for ways to increase the capacity of our weapons. When he came out against the Vietnam War, Dr. Martin Luther King once asked, 'How can I tell protesters not to use Molotov cocktails when our own government does much worse?'"

Is there reason to hope?, Gumbleton was asked. "Ultimately, hope is 'not by sight but by faith,' and that is how we live. Once you accept that Jesus is still alive within the church, that's your hope. As for more concrete signs that aren't based on faith, it *is* hard to find any because of the violence that seems out of control in this country. I see people talking all the time about introducing common sense into gun control, but even the president isn't taking any real steps because violence is so ingrained in our culture.

"That's civil society. Within the church, you see hope in Francis because he's much more open, saying everyone is welcome in the church and even atheists are in heaven—that sort of thing. But local parishes are being closed all over the country, even parishes of three hundred people, because we say they're too small. The real problem is that we won't deal with the priest shortage. There's also a loss of trust in the bishops and in the church due to financial mismanagements like the Vatican bank scandal and the sex abuse scandal.

"The church doesn't have the credibility it had when I was a kid. Young people don't have the allegiance to the church—especially to its leadership—that used to be there. Until we have a real transformation of church leadership, we need to hope that the presence of Jesus will show us the way, even though I can't see it right now with my limited human capacity."

The interview in *America* was classic Gumbleton: prophetic, calling for change, yet rooted in the institutions and structures of the church. He was, as always, willing to call out the church's shortcomings, its temptation to quietly slink into corners where it could concern itself with internal issues and fail to live out its prophetic function.

Bill O'Brien, a long-time Detroit community organizer, said that Gumbleton brought together disparate groups to work on common issues. O'Brien was active in Central American protest organizations, and found that Gumbleton was invaluable in bringing together Catholic pacifists with those who objected to U.S. policies in El Salvador in the 1980s.

O'Brien, a former Jesuit, said that Gumbleton's regular visits to Central America helped bring the news to American Catholics about the heroic struggles of Archbishop Oscar Romero against the military regime in El Salvador. "Gumbleton was bringing hope that the Catholic Church could be a church of the poor," he recalled.[7]

More than thirty years later, that became a regular theme of Pope Francis, an indication to Gumbleton's supporters that what he had been preaching had always been a central focus of gospel teaching. Now the church was recognizing it more explicitly. What had been couched in sometimes difficult to discern church documents was now part of the regular preaching of Pope Francis. But Gumbleton never needed to wait for official Vatican sanction or permission.

According to O'Brien, Gumbleton brought persistence to his causes. And courage as well. He remembered eating breakfast with the auxiliary bishop the morning after his testimony on sex abuse legislation at the Ohio legislature. Gumbleton knew that he had stirred the waters and would pay a price. "That took as much courage as anything I ever saw him do," recalled O'Brien. Gumbleton, he said, exhibited courage "not only in front of worldly or secular power, but courage in the face of his own institution."[8]

Still, even if Gumbleton played the role of outsider, others saw his influence on other bishops, even if they never constituted a majority of American bishops.

Jesuit Father Tom Reese is perhaps the most experienced and astute observer of the Catholic hierarchy in America. Formerly the editor of *America,* the Jesuit news and opinion journal, and a columnist for Religion News Service, Reese is the author of books on the U.S. bishops' conference and the internal workings of the church. He says that Gumbleton may have been an outsider in many ways among his fellow bishops, but his impact surpassed those who earned greater prestige and power in their careers.

Reese sees Gumbleton as moving his fellow bishops toward a greater appreciation of the church's stance on peace and disarmament. When Archbishop John Roach, then-president

---

7. Bill O'Brien, phone interview with author, December 2018.
8. Ibid.

of the National Conference of Catholic Bishops, put Gumbleton on the "Challenge of Peace" pastoral committee alongside then-Bishop John J. O'Connor, it was a stroke of genius, he said. "He knew that if he had Gumbleton and O'Connor on the committee, anything the two agreed on would pass unanimously," said Reese.

In the wider body of bishops, Gumbleton's views on pacifism and nonviolence represented a significant minority that Roach wanted represented on the committee. And, while Gumbleton often gets little credit for political skills, he was able to win many floor votes on the debate of the document, winning over other bishops with his arguments.

On other issues, such as his support for discussing the matter of women's ordination, Gumbleton found little support from his fellow bishops, particularly after Pope John Paul II described it as a closed issue. But Reese noted that Gumbleton's work on gay issues was ahead of its time, and helped nudge the thinking of his fellow bishops. The "Always Our Children" pastoral, issued in 1997 and directed to the parents of gay children, was highly praised for its pastoral tone. But ultimately, noted Reese, Gumbleton "was a prophet, not a politician. He was way out front of his fellow bishops." Sometimes that meant that Gumbleton was largely alone. "When you are way out in the front, you can turn around and sometimes see that there's no one behind you," said Reese.

Reese sees Gumbleton's role as vital, even when he didn't get much support. He likened it to Paul's letter to the Galatians, which articulates how the church needs many gifts. Gumbleton was in a kind of church exile for many years, yet, as the church moved into the Francis era, Gumbleton's previous statements match up rather well with the current Vatican leadership. In his openness to gays and divorced and remarried Catholics, Francis has signaled that his viewpoint is often aligned with the auxiliary bishop of Detroit.[9]

---

9. Thomas Reese, interview with author, December 2018.

Bishop Gumbleton at a meeting of the U.S. Bishops' Conference.
Credit: Rick Reinhard

Tom Fox, the publisher of the *National Catholic Reporter*, said that the bishop's legacy will be especially found in his role with Pax Christi USA, the Catholic peace organization. His perseverance in the cause of pacifism, offering an alternative to Catholic just-war teaching, has been a gift to the church, according to Fox. "The Challenge of Peace" pastoral letter formally recognized pacifism as a legitimate Catholic stance, alongside just-war theory. Despite these advances, Gumbleton never accumulated great power within church structures. No one takes records seriously, but it is probable that Gumbleton served in one position—auxiliary bishop of Detroit—longer than anyone in modern church history, spanning the 1960s into the approaching 2020s. Seemingly stagnated in the church hierarchy, Gumbleton kept pushing his views. As a result, he is a bishop of historic significance, said Fox.[10]

And he would live long enough to see his views on peace—long regarded as lying on the outside fringe of church teaching—now resonating with Vatican officials in the era of Pope Francis.

Gumbleton "was a Pope Francis before there was a Pope Francis," said John Carr, longtime staffer to the U.S. bishops on justice and peace issues, and now a professor at Georgetown University. It was not just in his prophetic message that Gumbleton reflected Pope Francis's model of servant leadership. Gumbleton, who lived out of his rectory office for decades and who preferred, when attending bishops meetings in Washington or Baltimore, to stay at the YMCA rather than a top-flight hotel, had long set an example of what Pope Francis would call "a shepherd with the smell of the sheep."[11]

He was not discouraged when few followed his lead. John Carr joked that Gumbleton's interventions at national bishops' meetings tended to take the form of a request to strike the first

10. Tom Fox, interview with author, December 2018.
11. John Carr, interview with author, December 2018.

thirteen pages of a statement in favor of a simple declaration that Jesus called us to love our enemies. "That was not an argument that was likely to persuade, but it was right to remind everyone," said Carr.

Yet if Gumbleton sometimes lacked diplomatic skills, Carr noted, his pastoral sense was sharp. When Carr's sister came out as a lesbian, the family had its issues, particularly his father, an Irish Catholic from Minnesota's Twin Cities. Carr's father read an article by Gumbleton directed at parents of gay children, a response to Gumbleton's own family issues when his brother Dan came out. Carr said that the words had a profound effect on his father, and he suspects that Gumbleton's outreach to other parents of gay children had a quiet, supportive quality that will have a long-lasting impact on thousands of Catholic families around the country. "Is Dan going to hell?" the question raised by Gumbleton's mother, sparked a pastoral response that would resonate far beyond his own family.

Perhaps because he was so willing to talk with reporters, Gumbleton was generally the beneficiary of positive press. The auxiliary bishop could always be counted on for a view different from the average bishop's. He made good copy. In the conservative sectors of the Catholic media, however, Gumbleton emerged as a favorite whipping boy. Often they were willing to cut the bishop some slack on his actions around nuclear weapons, poverty, and civil rights, largely because those issues were, ultimately, rather standard Catholic social justice fare.

But when he became active on internal church issues, particularly on gay rights and support for ordaining women, that was a different matter. *The Wanderer*, the granddaddy of what are sometimes referred to as "ultra-orthodox" publications, often treated him like a heretic. Church Militant, a relative newcomer to the Catholic culture wars, has regularly blamed Gumbleton for helping create an atmosphere of tolerance for gay clergy in the Archdiocese of Detroit, a development they regularly deride as the root cause of the sex abuse crisis.

Sometimes, Gumbleton's fellow bishops have kept a wary distance. He has occasionally been banned from speaking in dioceses, even in cases where he was not going to address any controversial topic. In 2005, Bishop Alexander K. Sample forbade Gumbleton from speaking at a social action conference in the Diocese of Marquette. Sample (now the archbishop of Portland, Oregon) thought his fellow bishop was not Catholic enough and shouldn't be allowed to promote his views in his diocese.

"Given Bishop Gumbleton's very public position on certain important matters of Catholic teaching, specifically with regard to homosexuality and the ordination of women to the priesthood, it was my judgment that his presence in Marquette would not be helpful to me in fulfilling my responsibility," said Sample.

The *New Oxford Review*, a favorite of Catholic traditionalists, praised Sample, describing Gumbleton as a "prince of episcopal heterodoxy." In another editorial in 2005, the *Review* described Gumbleton as one who "believes in universal salvation (except possibly for orthodox Catholics), he believes that gay sex can be moral, and he believes in ordaining priestesses. . . . Were your editor the pope, he would have had Gumbleton defrocked long ago."[12]

Still, amidst the editorial thunderbolts, the *New Oxford Review* offered Gumbleton grudging respect. Contrasting him with other bishops who have changed their tune to advance under the succession of varied papacies, Gumbleton has never wavered. He is not that different in his viewpoints from when he first became a bishop at the tender age of thirty-eight. Dearden had advised his protégé simply to be himself, and few doubt that Gumbleton followed that counsel.

In the sometimes nasty world of internal church politics,

12. Anonymous, "Bishops Banning Bishops," *New Oxford Review*, December 2009.

public figures come and go, emerging and then receding in the public eye. The church is, notwithstanding its divine origins, a very human organization. Often a buzz is created around church leaders, with the implication being that they often don't live up to the ideals they preach. Sometimes that can come in the form of quiet allegations of sexual impropriety or lavish lifestyles more consistent with a corporate executive than with the life of a pastoral shepherd. With Gumbleton, that buzz of rumor and innuendo has never existed. Even in embracing controversial views, both friend and foe acknowledge that the auxiliary bishop of Detroit has led a simple, austere life devoted to the poor. He sought out parishes in the middle of one of America's harshest cities, where poverty is endemic and casual violence is too often a part of life.

At some point, Gumbleton surely could have obtained a sinecure, a more lavish lifestyle, some would say more befitting a Catholic bishop. But, even when ordered out of the austere and humble St. Leo's rectory, Gumbleton retreated to a spartan apartment a few miles away. Its furnishings can only be described as adequate, a simple one-bedroom dwelling in what is an emerging Detroit neighborhood, but still far from what other cities consider as gentrification. He is a regular at the nearby Coney Island, a Detroit chain of simple diners. He will order the soup of the day. The staff calls him Tom. It is one of his simple pleasures.

For John Carr, Gumbleton is a prophetic figure who had no scheme to enhance his own power, but whose influence was widely felt. "There was no grand plan. He was just a faithful follower of Christ who cared about people and the gospel," he said.[13]

Tom Reese sees Gumbleton in a similar light. "He was the bishop for the peace and justice community across the country," he said. Gumbleton's frequent speaking tours offered

---

13. John Carr, interview with author, December 2018.

encouragement to Catholics who saw him as a signal that the church cared about their issues. At a time when church statements seemed almost completely aligned with conservative political as well as moral principles, Gumbleton offered hope to those who felt that a concern for the poor and promoting a more peaceful foreign policy were quite congruent with Catholic tradition.

"He helped a lot of peace and justice people stay in the church," said Reese. All of Gumbleton's frequent quoting of church documents helped connect their issues to the very heart of Catholic social teaching. Ironically, the fact that Gumbleton never ascended beyond his status as an auxiliary in Detroit, helped cement his legacy. Early on, noted Reese, it was clear that he wasn't going to lead a diocese of his own. That reality freed him from the burdens of other bishops, who spend much of their time in administrative duties, dealing with pastors and budgets. It also spared him criticism that bishops face for sometimes having to make unpopular decisions, like closing parishes or disciplining popular pastors. Reese noted that leading a diocese in today's church is often a thankless task. Gumbleton was liberated from that responsibility. "He was quite free as an auxiliary bishop," said Reese. "It allowed him to play the prophetic card much more easily."[14]

Even his ideological opponents were willing to grant that Gumbleton maintained a steely resolve and consistency that were difficult to attack, even if they often went after his positions. "Despite his bizarre theology," wrote the *New Oxford Review*, "he has not been ambitious, and you've gotta respect that. For Gumbleton, the Gospel boils down to the Social Gospel, but he does appear to practice what he preaches."[15]

At the time of that editorial, Gumbleton was residing in his modest rectory office at St. Leo's Church. He slept on a futon on

---

14. Thomas Reese, interview with author, December 2018.
15. Anonymous, "Bishops Banning Bishops," 13.

the floor. Most of his rectory had been given over to new mothers to help them with their drug addictions.

And, as the *Review* acknowledged, "He's very generous to the poor." This was around the time, at the age of seventy-five, when Gumbleton would normally have been facing retirement. Yet, as of this writing, he continues the same humble, if prolific pace, now past his eighty-ninth birthday.

"Gumbleton appears to have a heart of gold to a fault," said the *New Oxford Review*, acknowledging that that, no doubt, "will count for something on Judgment Day."